TI A

DISCARD

SECRETS OF ANCIENT CULTURES

THE INCA

Activities and Crafts from a Mysterious Land

Arlette N. Braman

Illustrated by Michele Nidenoff

WILEY

John Wiley & Sons, Inc.

This book is printed on acid-free paper. ∞

Photograph credits: Page 6, copyright © 2001 by Dan Heller; Pages 23, 24, 80, and 82 copyright © 2002 by William Schilling.

Published by John Wiley & Sons, Inc., Hoboken, New Jersey
Published simultaneously in Canada

Design and production by Navta Associates, Inc.

The publisher and the author have made every reasonable effort to ensure that the experiments and activities in the book are safe when conducted as instructed but assume no responsibility for any damage caused or sustained while performing the experiments or activities in this book. Parents, guardians, and/or teachers should supervise young readers who undertake the experiments and activities in this book.

For general information about our other products and services, please contact our Customer Care Department within the United States at (800) 762-2974, outside the United States at (317) 572-3993 or fax (317) 572-4002.

Wiley also publishes its books in a variety of electronic formats. Some content that appears in print may not be available in electronic books. For more information about Wiley products, visit our web site at www.wiley.com.

ISBN 0-471-21980-0

Printed in the United States of America

10 9 8 7 6 5 4 3 2 1

To TJS,

Machu Picchu awaits!

CONTENTS

ACKNOWLEDGMENTS

A big thanks to Robert Templeman, Assistant Professor of Ethnomusicology, University of Cincinnati, for his help with Quechua phrases; Luis Morató-Peña for providing information about the Quechua language; Elena Fihman for quinoa information; Bonnie Hamre, South American Visitors' Guide, for her suggestions about Andean stew and other helpful information; Bill Schilling for his beautiful photos of the Inca ruins; Dan Heller for his Quechua girl photo; Kate Bradford, Hope Breeman, and Megan Burke for their terrific suggestions, as always; Jill Decker for her poem contribution; Ian Werth and to my kids, Callan and Abigail, for testing the activities and recipes in this book.

ARLETTE'S ART TIPS

Here are some tips that will help you with the activities in this book.

1 For the painting projects, it's helpful to use craft paintbrushes with different brush thicknesses. When painting small areas, use a brush with thin bristles. For large areas, use a brush with thicker bristles.

2 Save clean plastic applesauce or fruit cups to use as paint pots or for mixing two paint colors together. Also use these cups to hold water for moistening your fingers when working with clay. Keep paper towels around for spills!

3 When working with clay, tape plastic-coated freezer paper to your work surface. It's heavier than wax paper, won't tear as you work with the clay, and can be thrown away when you are finished. It also protects your work surface from clay, paint, glue, or anything you use for your projects.

4 Clay-modeling tools have different tips, and the shape of a tip will help you create a certain look for your sculpture. Use a pointed tip to add small details like eyes and mouth. A wide, flat tip helps to smooth a surface. A ridged tip can be used to press lines into the clay. A dull knife tips lets you cut out sections of clay that are not needed.

5 If you paint your clay projects, you can spray them with a glossy, clear, quick-drying acrylic finish to prevent the paint from chipping. Make sure you wait until the paint is completely dry before you spray. *Always* spray objects outside and *ask an adult* for help. The fumes are strong, so you never want to do it indoors.

6 Clay projects dry faster and evenly if you turn them occasionally so each side is eventually exposed.

7 Whenever you cook using a recipe, *always ask an adult* for help. Never use the stove or oven unless you have checked with an adult first. Follow all of the directions in a recipe carefully. The recipes in this book were modified to make them easier for kids to use.

8 Remember always to clean up after you're finished.

SECRETS OF
ANCIENT CULTURES

THE INCA

Introduction
THE ANCIENT INCA

The ancient Inca lived in the western portion of present-day South America from about A.D. 1200 until A.D. 1532, when they were conquered by the Spanish. As early as 5000 B.C., the early inhabitants established a more settled way of life rather than relying on hunting and gathering, which required moving to find food. As these people began to farm the land, the population grew. Although little is known about the Andean people who lived in this area before the Inca, historians believe that there were many diverse groups or tribes of people.

We know about the fascinating Inca civilization from written historical documents, such as observations made by the Spanish conquerors, and from information that the Inca told the Spanish. The Inca had no written language to document their own history. In the mid-1600s, Felipe Guaman Poma de Ayala, son of a Spanish father and Inca mother, wrote a 1,000-page letter to the king of Spain about the abuses the Inca endured at the hands of the Spanish. He provided detailed information about the Inca and drew hundreds of pictures that today serve as a visual reference to Inca life.

Archaeology (the scientific study of material remains, such as fossil relics, artifacts, and monuments of past human life and activities) is another way we have learned about the Inca.

Geography

The Inca empire covered an area of about 2,200 miles (3,500 kilometers). This vast area has three main geographical zones: the coastal desert, the highlands, and the jungle.

The warm coastal desert stretches almost the entire length of the area. Although mostly warm, the sea current along the coast causes a cool, misty fog that hangs over the desert at certain times of year. The desert was too dry to grow many plants, so the Inca living there developed irrigation systems that used water that flowed down from river valleys high in the mountains. The Inca also created sunken fields, called *puquois,* by digging down to near the water table. This provided more water for crops. The Inca who lived in this area grew cotton, squashes, beans, chili peppers, maize, guava, peanuts, and avocados.

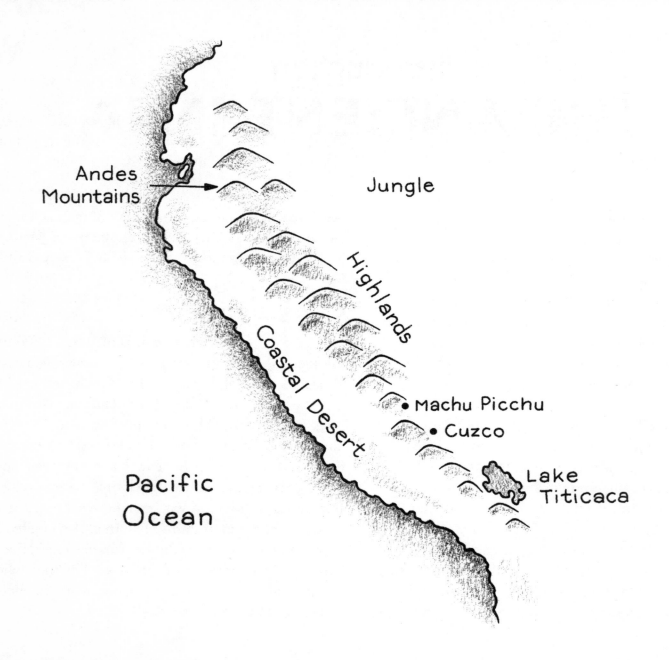

Andes
Mountains

Jungle

Highlands

Coastal Desert

● Machu Picchu

● Cuzco

Lake
Titicaca

Pacific
Ocean

The highlands are part of the Andes Mountains. The Inca grew crops, such as maize, chili peppers, and squash, in the highland valleys. At higher elevations, they grew potatoes, quinoa, and ocra. Llama, alpaca, and vicuña were herded on the high land surrounding the valleys, while deer and puma roamed wild. Some bodies of water in the highlands did not flow down to the sea. One such lake, Lake Titicaca, a sacred place to the Inca, is located between present-day Peru and Bolivia some 12,468 feet (2,800 m) above sea level. Another lake, located in present-day northern Chile, dried up many years ago and formed the Atacama desert.

The jungle is made up of the *montaña,* the sloped area of land between the highlands and the rain forest, and the *selva,* the rain forest that reaches to the Amazon Basin. These areas had the best conditions for growing many different fruits and vegetables, as well as coca, manioc, and tobacco. Deer, bears, tapirs, monkeys, jaguars, and snakes lived in the jungle.

Inca Empire

The Inca divided their empire into four quarters or provinces. The northwest was called *Chinchaysuyu;* the northeast, *Antisuyu;* the southwest, *Cuntisuyu;* and the southeast, *Collasuyu.* Cuzco, the capital, was located in the center of the empire, where the provinces met. The Inca called this land *Tahuantinsuyu,* which means "Land of the Four Quarters," in their native language, Quechua. Each quarter was further divided into provinces, totaling about eighty overall. The Inca army, highly organized and powerful, conquered many neighboring tribes and incorporated them into their empire, allowing for its enormous growth. The greatest expansion of their territory took place during the reign of the last four kings, from about A.D. 1438 to A.D. 1532. At the height of their dominance, the Inca numbered about 10 million.

Society

The Inca were organized into small, related social groups that were then integrated into larger organizational units. *Ayllu* was the word used to describe the basic organizational group. Members of an ayllu were usually related, but the Inca occasionally organized a group of unrelated people into an ayllu if they needed a group to live in a certain part of the empire for work or tax reasons.

Inca society consisted of three major groups. The Inca ruler and his immediate family ranked at the top. Government officials made up the next group. Workers, who were the taxpayers, made up the third largest group. Everyone in the empire had a certain role to fill and stayed within their social class, which was determined at birth. People were kept busy with work, no matter what their rank.

When neighboring tribes were captured, their people were integrated into the Inca empire. However, the Inca believed it was better to let these captured people maintain their own way of living. This caused less disruption among the people and helped them adjust better to being under the Inca's rule.

The Inca expected these people to work for the empire and become loyal subjects. Captured leaders were allowed to hold local government positions and continue to practice their own religions. Sons of captured leaders were brought to Cuzco, where they learned about Inca policies and government. When an older captured leader died, his son would take over and govern according to Inca beliefs.

Cuzco

Cuzco was home to 15,000 to 20,000 people. When Pachacuti Inca became ruler in 1438, he redesigned the city in the shape of a puma, an important animal to the Inca. Like the empire, Cuzco was divided into four quarters. Pachacuti Inca had two

WHAT'S IN A NAME?

We now refer to all of the people who lived in the Inca Empire during this time as *Inca*. But the ancient Inca referred to the king as *Sapa Inca,* which meant "Unique Inca" or "Only Inca," and called all of his relatives Inca. Another group of people, called *Inca by Privilege,* were considered part of the upper class. The Inca by Privilege were not Inca by birth, but inherited the title because they had lived in the Cuzco region before becoming part of the empire and were Quechua-speaking allies of the Inca. All other people in the empire were not allowed to call themselves Inca. They were referred to as *the common people* or *taxpayers*.

major canals built and had the most important buildings, including temples, palaces, schools for noble children, and administrative buildings, constructed around the canals in the central plaza, called the *Huacapata.* The Huacapata was the key part of the city and was where the Inca celebrated important events. From this plaza, four roads led to the city's four quarters. The Inca referred to Cuzco as the "navel" of the world.

Only the king and the powerful nobles, including priests and high-ranking government officials, and servants of these nobles, lived in Cuzco. Provincial governors and lower-ranking officials lived in the provincial capitals, which were laid out much like Cuzco, only on a smaller scale. Throughout the empire, the lower classes lived farther away from the cities in more rural areas.

Language

The native language of the Inca was *Quechua* (KECH-wah). It is still spoken by the native people living in Peru today, but in many different dialects across the country. The ancient Inca had difficulty communicating with captured people, who were allowed to continue speaking their own languages. It is believed that these people were made to learn Quechua from *mitimaes,* large groups of Inca who were transplanted to an area where newly conquered people lived. This was the most efficient way to teach new people the language. As newly captured people learned Quechua, they were expected to teach it to their children.

Here are a few simple Quechua phrases to try:

English: "What's your name?"

Quechua: *"Imata sutiky?"*
Pronunciation: (Ee-MAH-tah sue-TEE-key)

English: "My name is . . ."

Quechua: "(Your name) *sutiyoq"*
Pronunciation: (Sue-TEE-yak) In Quechua the person says his or her name first. An example is: "Mary sutiyoq" which means "Mary is my name."

English: "How are you?"

Quechua: *"Imanaya kashanki?"*
Pronunciation: (Ee-mah-NAY-yah kah-SHAN-key)

English: "I am fine."

Quechua: *"Walequia kashani."*
Pronunciation: (Wah-LEH-key-ya kah-SHAN-ee)

Myths

Myths were an important part of Inca life. Myths were used to explain Inca religion, customs, and moral codes. There are a number of oral versions of the origin myth that were later written down by the Spanish. According to one, the Sun, the Moon, and the world were created by Viracocha, the god of Creation, from the Isle of the Sun in Lake Titicaca. After a great flood, Viracocha came to earth and created animals, plants, and men. He created the city of Tiahuanaco and appointed four rulers, one of whom was Manco Capac, who eventually founded the city of Cuzco and became the first Inca ruler.

The Spanish Conquest

In 1532, the Spanish explorer Francisco Pizarro and a group of 180 **conquistadors** (people who conquer), arrived in Inca territory. Pizarro first went to present-day Colombia in 1509 in search of new lands for the king of Spain. Once in this new world, he discovered that the native people had an abundance of gold, precious stones, and other treasures. He conducted many expeditions in search of these items, and he was eventually led to Inca lands.

About the time Pizarro arrived, the Inca empire was already beginning to weaken because its territory had become too large to manage. The Inca had more and more difficulty putting down rebellious tribes, especially those in the remote jungle areas in the east. When the Inca king Huayna Capac died in 1525 without having named a successor, a bitter fight began between two of his sons, Huascar and Atahuallpa, over who would succeed their father as king. The fight plunged the empire into a civil war that seriously strained the empire. Huascar was captured and imprisoned, and Atahuallpa took over.

When Atahuallpa received the news that Pizarro had arrived, he was not very concerned about this stranger because he knew he had a large army to defeat Pizarro's small group of men. Atahuallpa received and accepted an invitation to meet with Pizarro, and he went to Cajamarca, where Pizarro was staying. When Atahuallpa arrived with his army, only a few Spaniards met with him, including the Bishop Vincente de Valverde, who asked the Inca leader to accept the Christian faith. Atahuallpa refused and was attacked by the rest of Pizarro's men, who had been hiding. The element of surprise and the Spanish weapons, including guns, led to the king's capture. The Inca had no guns to use against Pizarro and his men.

Atahuallpa was held for ransom, and his people paid more than 50 million U.S. dollars in gold by today's standards for his release. Atahuallpa was not freed but instead was strangled by the Spaniards who had captured him. The Spanish captured Cuzco, put Inca rulers in place who had sworn allegiance to the Spanish, and then began to steal much of the Inca's gold and silver. During the long period of Spanish domination, great numbers of Inca died from diseases, such as smallpox and influenza, that the Spaniards carried. Not having been exposed to these diseases before, the Inca had no natural resistance to them. Many of the captured Inca who survived had to work on the plantations and in the silver and gold mines, which were abundant throughout the empire and run by the Spaniards. The Inca resisted Spanish control and continued to fight for fifty years after the conquest. A number of Inca rulers tried to regain power, but were not successful. The last reigning Inca, Túpac Amaru, was captured in 1572 by the Spaniards and beheaded in a public ceremony in Cuzco.

Descendants of the Inca

There are more than 12 million people today living in Peru, Bolivia, Ecuador, Argentina, Brazil, and Chile who are

descended from the ancient Inca. Many still speak Quechua, the language of the Inca. They have learned to blend modern ways with traditional practices. Many practice both Christianity and the traditional Inca religion. Many wear traditional clothing, but also add modern touches, like wool sweaters. Many farmers continue to use the traditional Inca farming methods, such as terraced farming, and women weave beautiful textiles with a backstrap loom as their ancestors did. Most children are taught traditional Inca ways and values even today.

SOCIETY

Everyone in Inca society belonged to a particular social group. At the top was the Inca king and the royal family. The king was the absolute ruler and needed a well-organized government to rule over such a large empire. Next came the four *apus,* the officials who governed the four quarters, and their families. The apus were probably related to the king and worked closely with him. Below the apus in rank came the governors of the provinces, who managed the 80 provinces across the 4 quarters. These governors reported directly to the apus. Reporting to these governors were the *curacas,* officials who managed the households in the provinces. Because there were so many households in the empire, five levels of curacas were needed. The highest-level curacas were responsible for 10,000 households, while the lowest-level curacas managed 100 households. Each level of curacas reported directly to the curacas above them. The *camayocs* were next and had the task of acting as district leaders, managing smaller areas of the provinces.

All of these people made up one large social group, considered the upper class, but they were organized into different levels within this group. The king held the highest, most noble position, while the *curacas* and *camayocs* held the lowest position. Priests, architects, engineers, artisans, and members of the army were included in this social group. They ranked below the king but above the *curacas* and *camayocs.*

The largest group of people, the commoners, or tax-payers, ranked at the bottom of the pyramid. Most of the people in this rank were farmers, followed by people who worked at a trade, such as metalworking, pottery, stone-cutting, or weaving. This group of people paid taxes in the form of labor, called *mit'a.*

ROYAL EDICT

The Inca king imposed a labor tax program called a *mit'a* on the common people. It took farmers far less than a year to grow enough crops to feed their families. During the rest of the year, farmers, as well as other labor-ers such as fishermen, stonecutters, and herdsmen, had to work on the government-owned fields, help construct temples, build roads and bridges, and mine for gold and silver. Sometimes groups of people were relocated if they were not busy enough in their regular location. The king always wanted people to be busy but made sure that everyone, including the workers, had enough food to keep them happy, healthy, and working hard.

CRIME AND PUNISHMENT

The Inca had many different kinds of laws. There were laws governing agriculture, laws to distribute work fairly, laws that covered how many possessions a common person might own, and a law that helped those in need, such as the elderly and disabled.

Laws were enforced by Inca government officials throughout the empire. Smaller crimes were handled by the various levels of curacas, and more serious crimes were handled by provincial governors. Inca provincial governors were allowed to order the death sentence if they believed the crime was a serious offense. Commoners were punished more severely than nobles for similar crimes. A noble might endure public humiliation, but a commoner might receive the death sentence.

Punishments ranged from death for stealing food from any field, whether it was the king's, the gods', or the com-mon people's, to having a large stone dropped on one's back from a height of about 3 feet (1 m) for a lower-ranking curaca who did not get the proper permission before making a decision. One unpleasant punishment was confinement in an underground pit filled with poisonous snakes.

Division of Land

Inca farmland was divided into three parts. One part belonged to the king, another to the gods, and the last part to the local farming communities. All harvested food was placed in storehouses located throughout the empire. Food was distributed to all the people so that everyone had enough to eat. Crops grown on the king's land supported the king, his family, and the nobles. Crops grown on the gods' land fed the priests and attendants of the shrines and were offered to the gods. Food grown for the farming communities was used for the common people. Farmers were responsible for farming all the land, not just their own.

KINGS

The Inca king was believed to be descended from Inti, the Sun god, and the people viewed the king as a god on earth. The king usually married another descendent of the Sun god. Often this person was his sister. She was known as the *Coya.* The king was allowed to marry many wives, but only the Coya produced suitable heirs to the throne. The king selected one of his sons to follow in his footsteps. This honor did not always go to the first-born son, but to the one who showed the most promise as a good ruler.

Noble Privileges

Running such a vast empire required a great deal of help. All of the officials who assisted the king through-out the empire were part of this "noble class." Army officers and priests were usually recruited from this class. High-ranking nobles enjoyed many privileges, although never as many as the king. They wore fancy clothes and rode in **litters** (chairs with poles attached, used for carrying important people). They could wear beautiful gold

INCA KINGS

According to historical records, the Inca had thirteen kings, but the first eight may have only been legends.

1. Manco Capac is considered the legendary founder of the Inca people.
2. Sinchi Roca was a peaceful ruler.
3. Lloque Yupanqui also believed in peace.
4. Mayta Capac created bad feelings among the people, and a rebellion began.
5. Capac Yupanqui made small conquests in the area.
6. Inca Roca also conquered neighboring tribes.
7. Yahuar Huacac continued to conquer neighboring tribes.
8. Viracocha Inca was the first ruler to use the title Sapa Inca.
9. Pachacuti Inca Yupanqui saw a great expansion of the empire under his rule and made Quechua the official language of the Inca in 1438.
10. Topa Inca Yupanqui continued to expand the empire.
11. Huayna Capac also continued expansion and first heard of bearded strangers who had arrived on the coast. He did not name an heir before his death.
12. Huascar was Huayna Capac's son. He fought Atahuallpa, his brother, for the throne after their father's death.
13. Atahuallpa was the son of Huayna Capac who succeeded in claiming the throne. He had his brother, Huascar, put to death.

After Atahuallpa, six more royals either tried to regain power or were appointed as temporary rulers by the Spaniards. But none were successful, and the Inca empire ultimately came under Spanish rule.

earplugs. The king gave them llamas, servants, land, and, sometimes, extra wives. The nobles never had to pay taxes. Everything they needed, they received from the government.

A Day in the Life

The king's life was one of privilege and comfort. Although he dressed in the same style of clothing as his subjects, his clothes were made from finer cloth. According to Spanish documents, the king never wore the same outfit twice. His previously worn clothes were either burned or handed down to his relatives. He ate his meals from bowls made of gold and silver. Servants who brought the king his food had to remove their sandals before entering his room. Few of these servants actually saw the king up close. He sat behind a screen while only one or two specially selected servants handed him his food. He slept on top of a thick, comfortable cotton quilt on the floor and covered himself with warm woolen blankets.

The king visited different parts of his empire to meet with the provincial governors and other regional officials to discuss government business and to make sure that the common people were working efficiently. He traveled in a beautiful litter made of gold and decorated with precious stones and colorful bird feathers. Many people accompanied the king on these travels. Runners would announce his arrival, road cleaners cleared the path for the approaching litter, which up to 20 men carried to insure a smooth ride, and guards went along to keep him safe. While he was away from Cuzco, he stayed in specially built houses that were constructed throughout the empire for his use. These houses were spaced about 12 miles (20 km) apart so he could stop and rest if he needed. Back in Cuzco, the king met with his highest-ranking officials to discuss day-to-day business, pass laws, entertain visiting dignitaries, prepare for war, or conduct ceremonies.

When a king died, it was believed that his father, the Sun god, had taken him back. People mourned his death for one year. After death, the king's body was preserved, possibly with a variety of herbs, and was then wrapped in cloth. His body was kept in the palace where he had lived, and his servants and wives continued to take care of it by bringing him daily food and offerings, such as cloth. During public ceremonies, such as the Sun Festival, his body was carried in a litter in the open plaza so people could worship him.

The Heir

The king selected one of his legitimate sons to reign as the king after his death. The legitimate sons were those whose mother was the Coya. The selected son was trained early in life for this role by going to school to learn about Inca history, oral literature, geometry, basic math, engineering, and how to read a **quipu** (a method of record keeping using knotted strings). He also learned about war and received physical and strategic training. After he completed tests of skill as an athlete and warrior against other nobles' sons, he was knighted and was expected to take part in military conquests.

THE COYA

As the main wife and full sister of the king, the Coya also lived a privileged life. While her husband was busy with government business, she was busy with other duties, including tending her garden, participating in religious festivals, and developing the public's interest in the arts and entertainment, such as poetry readings. The Coya lived in her own palace in Cuzco and had her own coat of arms, a rainbow, painted at the entrance of her palace. She had servants who helped her bathe twice a day, helped her dress, and accompanied her on daily walks.

ROYAL RELAXATION

The king would sometimes relax by soaking in a sunken stone bath in the palace. Spring water from a mountain ran down through stone channels into the bath.

ROYAL HEADDRESS

One of the most important royal symbols was the royal headdress, called the *llauta.* The llauta was made of colorful braids of woolen yarn that were wrapped around the forehead. The royal fringe, called the *borla,* consisted of tassels that were hung in little gold tubes from the front of the braid and rested on the forehead. The fringe was made from vicuña wool that had been dyed red. The king's heir wore a yellow fringe. A small silver or gold ornament was placed in the center front of the headdress and supported three feathers. The king wore this headdress for all important occasions, when meeting other important people, and when involved with any government business.

In this activity, you will create an Inca headdress in the same style of the royal headdress.

STEPS

1 Wrap a piece of yarn around your head 2 times. Cut 12 strands of yarn in a variety of colors at this same length.

2 Hold all the strands together, lining up the edges. Using a small piece of yarn, tie a tight knot around one end of the strands. Tape the knotted end to your work surface. Divide the strands into 3 groups of 4 strands each.

3 To braid the yarn, place the left group of strands over the middle group of strands, then place the right group of strands over the new middle group of strands (original left group). Repeat this step by placing the new left group of strands over the new middle group of strands, then the new right group of strands over the new middle group of strands, as shown.

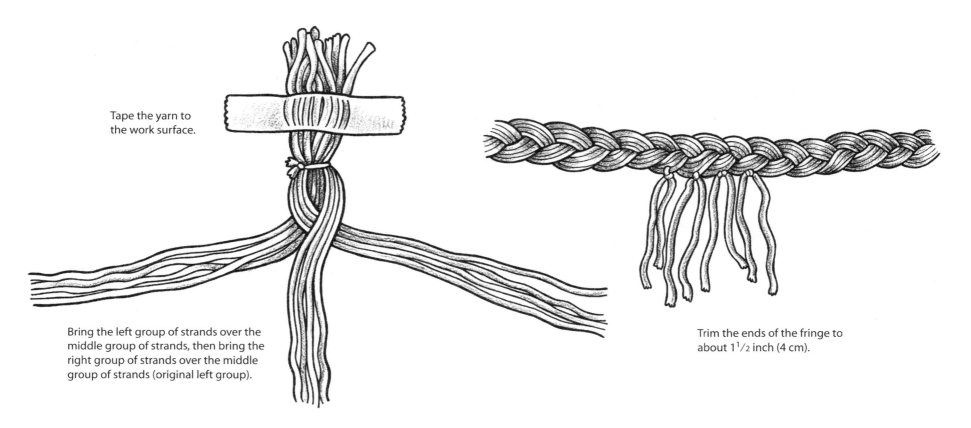

Tape the yarn to the work surface.

Bring the left group of strands over the middle group of strands, then bring the right group of strands over the middle group of strands (original left group).

Trim the ends of the fringe to about 1¹/₂ inch (4 cm).

4   When you reach the end, tie a tight knot around it using a small piece of yarn. Place the braid around your forehead and tie it at the back of your head to check the fit.

5   To make the fringe across the front of the headband, cut 10 pieces of red yarn that are each 4 inches (10 cm) long. Tie each piece of yarn to the headband so that the pieces are spaced evenly apart along the front side only.

You want them to rest on your forehead. Trim the fringe to about 1¹/₂ inches (4 cm).

6   Cut a circle with a diameter of about 3 inches (8 cm) from the foil. *Ask an adult* to help you use the tip of the scissors to poke two small holes about 1 inch (2.5 cm) apart and about ¹/₂ inch (1.5 cm) up from the bottom of the circle. Cut a piece of yarn about 12 inches (31 cm) long. Poke the two ends of the yarn through the front

holes in the foil. Center the foil circle over the front of the headband, poke the two yarn ends through the braid, and then tie the yarn ends in a knot to secure the foil in place. Stick three feathers into the top of the braid, just behind the foil circle.

ome kings had a **coat of arms** (identifying crest or emblem) on their litters. These symbols were often made of gold, silver, and precious stones. The most common coats of arms were the Sun, the Moon, or serpents intertwined around a staff.

ROYAL MEDALLION

Another symbol of royal status was a gold or silver medallion that hung from a cord and was worn around the neck. The king wore this medallion for all important public ceremonies, when he greeted important visitors, and when he traveled throughout his empire. The medallion usually had the image of Inti, the Sun god, hammered into the metal. In this activity, you will create a medallion you can wear with your headdress.

SUPPLIES

- 1 piece of oak tag, 10 by 10 inches (25 by 25 cm)
- pencil
- ruler
- scissors
- embossing foil in gold or silver, a few sheets or 1 small roll
- masking tape
- paint brush
- 1 strand of yarn, about $2^1/_2$ feet (77 cm)

STEPS

1 Draw an oval that measures about 5 by 7 inches (13 by 18 cm) on the oak tag. Cut out the oval.

2 Measure and cut a piece of foil that is larger than the oak tag oval by about 2 inches (5 cm) all around.

3 Lay the foil oval facedown on your work surface. Place the oak tag oval on the foil oval and bend the foil edges up over the edge of the oak tag oval. Tape the edges of the foil to the oak tag oval.

4 Turn the medallion over so the foil side faces up and make facial features, such as eyes, a nose, and a mouth, by pressing lightly with the blunt rounded end of the paint brush.

5 *Ask an adult* to help you use the tip of the scissors to poke two holes, spaced about an inch (2.5 cm) apart, through the top of the medallion.

6 Push one end of the yarn through the holes, then tie the two ends in a tight knot. Wear the royal medallion around your neck.

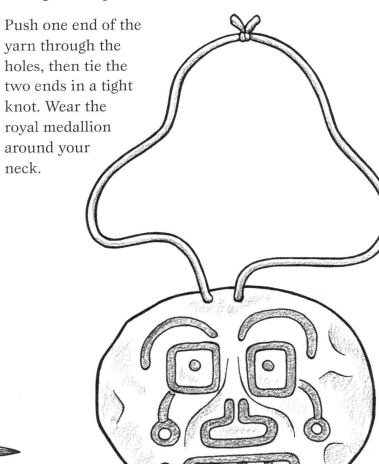

Press the foil with the rounded end of the paint brush to make the facial features.

WARRIORS

The Inca had a large, well-organized army of foot soldiers that was commanded by smart leaders. From boyhood, males were trained in war games and learned how to use weapons. Only the king's army, which consisted of a few thousand warriors and captains, was a permanent army. The regular army was made up of soldiers who were called to duty as needed. These soldiers may have had other jobs in the empire, but like all Inca men between the ages of twenty-five and fifty, they were expected to serve in the military. The early Inca defended their homeland by conducting raids on neighboring territories and successfully conquering the people who lived there. Over time, the Inca army grew and became powerful enough to defeat most enemy armies it encountered. Occasionally, the Inca didn't attack an enemy, but instead tried to persuade them to surrender. Sometimes this tactic worked. If not, an attack followed. Conquered warriors often became part of the Inca military, and the people of conquered lands became part of the Inca empire.

Weapons

Warriors used simple weapons, such as spears, swords, battle-axes, and clubs, which were made by attaching a stone to the end of a piece of wood. Sometimes the stone was shaped like a star with bronze or copper points sticking out. Warriors also used a slingshot made of rawhide or wood to shoot rocks over a long distance. The *bola,* a leather strap with rocks secured at the ends, could be flung at an enemy in such a way that it wrapped around the enemy's legs, causing him to fall. With his legs bound, he could not run to safety. Inca warriors from the tropical regions used bows and arrows. Those on the coast used spears and darts. Thick, quilted cotton tunics served as armor. Warriors carried wooden and metal shields and also wore them on their backs over their tunics for added protection. They all wore helmets made of wood or quilted cotton.

FEEDING THE TROOPS

The Inca not only had to provide food for this large army, but they had to distribute the food over an enormous area. To do this, they constructed an extensive road system that connected many parts of the empire and established buildings at strategic locations for food storage. These storage locations also contained extra weapons and clothing.

Going into Battle

Once a decision was made to go into battle, the troops were organized and the generals met to plan attack strategies. The king often led the troops into battle but always rode in his litter and was well protected by the generals and warriors. Priests gave each warrior a sacred object, or charm, as added protection and accompanied the troops to pray for a successful battle. To signal the start of a battle, some warriors played war music with trumpets, flutes, and drums. The king rewarded acts of bravery with gifts, including woven cloth or even extra wives if the warrior held a high-ranking position.

Warriors tried to either capture or kill enemy soldiers. If a warrior succeeded in killing an opponent, he could keep the body. Some warriors used enemy skulls as bowls, made flutes from their shinbones, and made necklaces from their teeth. These objects symbolized the greatness of the warrior. If an enemy ruler was captured, he might be sacrificed, or killed, if he did not agree to live by Inca rule.

WAR SHIELD

All warriors carried square or round shields made from wood covered with metal or deerskin. A piece of cloth decorated with a painted or woven emblem hung over the front of the shield. No one knows for sure what these emblems stood for, but it is believed that they may have been an identifying regional mark or design. Warriors' clothes also contained these designs.

Make your own shield and decorate it with Inca designs or with your own designs.

SUPPLIES

- heavy cardboard, 16 inches by 10 inches (41 by 25 cm)
- 1 piece of cardboard, 8 by 3 inches (20 by 8 cm)
- duct tape
- pencil
- acrylic paint in a variety of colors, such as red, blue, brown, yellow, and black
- paintbrush

STEPS

1 Using the pencil, draw some designs on the front of the heavy cardboard. For design ideas, look at the Inca shields pictured on page 20 and the finished shield at the end of this activity.

2 Turn the shield facedown and place the small piece of cardboard about ¹/₃ of the way down from the top edge of the shield. Tape the two short edges to the back of the shield using the duct tape. You should be able to slide your hand under this piece of cardboard to hold your shield.

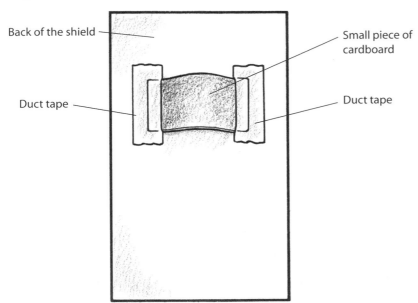

Back of the shield

Small piece of cardboard

Duct tape

Duct tape

3 Turn the shield faceup and paint your design. Let the paint dry completely.

FARMERS

Inca farmers were masters at agriculture and irrigation. Much of the empire was in the highlands, so just solving the problem of irrigating the crops was an engineering feat. The ingenious Inca built a series of stone **canals** (artificial waterways used for draining or irrigating land) to bring mountain spring water to the crops. While the Inca did not develop the irrigation system they used, they did improve it and brought it to a more sophisticated level than earlier civilizations. The Inca developed two different types of canals. In the slopes at the higher elevations, the Inca made masonry canals out of stones set in mud **mortar** (a mixture of cement, lime, sand, and water that hardens and is used as a plaster). This type of canal worked better on curved surfaces because it could follow the curve of the slope. In towns, on flatter surfaces, the Inca laid bricks made of **adobe** (a brick or building material made of sun-dried earth and straw) end to end to create long, straight canals.

Once this job had been completed, planting rituals, including ceremonies to the gods asking for a successful growing season, were conducted in August. In September, maize and potatoes were planted. The Inca planted potatoes in the highlands and maize, or corn, in the lowlands, on the slopes, and in the low valleys of the highlands. Inca farmers often grew more than 150 varieties of potatoes in a single field. Coca, important for its use in religious rituals, was planted in December in the wet lowlands. Farmers waited until the first signs of growth appeared, then began weeding and irrigating the fields until the rains came in January. Some potatoes were harvested in March, and the rest were harvested in June. Maize was harvested in May. If all went well, harvesting season was a time to rejoice.

The Life of a Farmer

Most Inca were farmers because many farmers were needed to grow enough crops to feed all the people in the empire. Before crops could grow, the farmers had to prepare the fields. The fields belonging to the king and to the gods were prepared first, and community fields were prepared last. Both men and women prepared the fields. Men used pointed digging sticks called *taclla* to break the ground into chunks, and then women used a wooden stick weighted at one end with a stone ring to divide these chunks into smaller pieces.

RAIN RITUAL

If the rains were late or infrequent, the people held a ritual asking the Thunder god to release the rains. They asked him to break the jar that held the rain water. If this didn't work, the Inca tied up black dogs and black llamas and didn't feed them, hoping their cries would convince the Thunder god to bring the rains.

HANDY CARRYALL

With no wheeled vehicles, men and women had to carry sacks of potatoes on their backs to the storehouses. To make this as easy as possible, the Inca wore a sling that crossed over the forehead, then hung down the back. The sack of potatoes sat in the sling against the person's back.

Hillside Farming

Because the highland Inca lived in mountainous terrain, they built terraces, or steps, into the slopes of the land for crop planting. Doing so enabled the Inca to use as much land as possible. The Inca also learned that they could plant more crops in terraced fields than in flat fields. Engineers designed the terrace walls so that they followed the natural curves of the hillside. Establishing the terraced fields required many mit'a workers.

PLANT A POTATO

The potato, called *papa* by the Inca, is a hearty **tuber** (fleshy edible root crop) that had its beginning in the Andes. Potatoes are not grown from seeds. They grow from the eyes of other potatoes. The eye is the white bud that grows out of the potato. Try your hand at farming and plant a potato as the Inca did. *Note: You will not eat the potatoes you grow. This activity is to see the growing process only. Potatoes grown and sold by farmers are carefully monitored for diseases and pests.*

SUPPLIES

- 1 potato with eyes
- 1 knife
  Note: Ask an adult for help before using the knife.
- 1 plate
- potting soil
- 1 flowerpot with drainage holes and saucer. The pot's opening should be 10 to 12 inches (25 to 30 cm)
- 1 garden spade or small hand shovel

STEPS

1 Make sure the potato has eyes sticking out of it. The eyes do not have to be very long.

2 Cut the potato into 3 or 4 chunks. Each chunk should have one or two eyes on it. Place the potato chunks on the plate and let them sit out overnight.

3 Fill the bottom of the pot with about 2 inches (5 cm) of soil. Place the potato chunks on the soil with some space in between each piece, then cover them with

about 1 inch (2.5 cm) of soil. Water the soil but don't let it get soggy.

4 Place the pot in a sunny spot and watch for sprouts. Once the sprouts begin to grow, place more soil around the base of their stems. Build up the soil at the base to support the stem but don't bury the sprout.

5 Water the sprouts when the soil begins to dry out. Do not let the soil dry out completely. You want to keep it moist but not soggy.

6 After about 8 weeks, the sprouts will have grown into potatoes. You can dig up the new potatoes by carefully sliding the shovel down along the inside of the pot and gently scooping out the potatoes. Brush the dirt off the potatoes.

TWO CALENDARS

The Inca developed two calendars. The solar, or daytime, calendar was like our calendar and had 365 days. It is believed that this calendar was used mainly for determining the timing of agricultural activities, such as planting, irrigating, weeding, and harvesting.

The lunar, or nighttime, calendar was created to determine when important festivals that were associated with the phases of the moon would occur.

EVERYDAY LIFE

The average Inca spent a large part of the day working for the empire as weavers, farmers, sewers, road and bridge builders, and stonecutters. The upper classes worked, too, but had different jobs, such as provincial governor, military leader, architect, priest, and assistant to the king. Life was busy and demanding, and people were not allowed to enjoy much idle time.

The Family Home

Each of the 80 provinces included about 20,000 households, which might include a mother, father, children, grandparents, aunts, and uncles. Inca homes differed slightly in design according to their location. In the highlands, homes were built of stone and had sloped roofs made of **thatch** (any type of plant material used as a cover). In the coastal areas, walls were made of adobe that was coated with a layer of mud plaster. The average Inca house generally had one room with no furniture.

beans, squash, chili peppers, yams, and **quinoa** (an Andes region plant whose seeds are ground and used as food). Other important foods included peanuts, tomatoes, a grain called *tarwi,* and an edible root called *oca.* The Inca occasionally ate meat, though not on a daily basis. Most foods were either boiled in a large pot or roasted over an open fire. Fruits, such as bananas, papayas, plums, and avocados, were also a part of the Inca diet.

The Inca who lived along the coast and near Lake Titicaca included fish in their diet. Many of the Inca who lived along the coast worked as fishermen for the government.

After the Spanish conquest, the Inca incorporated new foods into their diet, such as beef, chicken, rabbit, wheat, apples, peaches, oranges, limes, and cherries. Sugarcane provided a whole new taste for the Inca. They had used honey to sweeten foods.

Family Meals

The Inca ate two meals a day. The morning meal was the most important. The second meal was eaten at dusk. During meals, the women sat facing the cooking pots with their backs to the men. The average Inca used simple plates and cups made from wood or pottery. Nobles ate from plates made of gold and silver and had their food prepared by servants.

Meals consisted of any combination of corn, potatoes,

Raising Children

A few days after birth, babies were placed in wooden cradles where they spent most of their time until they could walk. These cradles were portable and could be moved to wherever the mother went to work.

When a child was too big for the cradle, its mother dug a hole in the ground as deep as the child's chest and placed the child in the hole, which was lined with blankets. The child would play in this hole while the mother worked.

The Inca did not name their new babies until they were between one to two years old. At that time, the parents held a ceremony where the oldest male relative cut a piece of the baby's hair and gave the baby a temporary name. At puberty, the child received his or her permanent name.

Young children learned to help out at home. Girls helped take care of the younger children and learned how to cook and weave. Boys took care of the animals, collected firewood, and kept predators away from the fields. When they were about 12 years old and considered strong enough, boys were sent to the fields each day to help with farming. Boys from noble families, those in the highest levels of the upper class, attended four years of school in Cuzco, where they learned Quechua, religion, quipu use, and Inca history. After they passed their final exams, they had their ears pierced and wore gold earplugs, a sign of nobility.

Teenagers were considered ready for marriage: girls between 16 and 20, and boys between 18 and 25. They had to find a partner from their own ayllu, and when they did, they needed permission from a local curaca to marry. A man, accompanied by his parents, went to the home of his selected bride to give her a sandal for her right foot. He took her hand, and then everyone went to his parents' house, where the woman gave her prospective husband a woolen shirt she had woven for him. Both sets of parents stayed until nightfall talking to their children about how to treat their prospective spouses in marriage. The next day, the curaca married the two people. Both sets of relatives celebrated by feasting and drinking. The community built the new couple a home to help them get started. (For newly married noble couples, the house was built by the mit'a.)

Death

The Inca believed that after death, people went to live in another world. Very good people went to live with the Sun in the upper world, called *Hanac-paca*. People who had not lived a good life went to the interior of the earth, where they were always cold and hungry. Inca nobility always went to live with the Sun god no matter how they had lived their lives. Bodies were buried in tombs. Some tombs were built against cliffs or in large rock shelters, while others were freestanding round or square structures made of adobe bricks. The deceased was placed in a sitting position, wrapped in cloth, then placed in the tomb with different objects, including baskets, pottery, food, jewelry, and something very personal; for example, fishermen were buried with their fishing gear, while a weaver was buried with her weaving tools.

Burial Figurines

When children died their relatives made human figurines and buried them with the bodies. The Inca believed that these figurines acted as companions to the children. The Inca took great care in dressing the figurines. Royal children got exquisitely dressed figurines, while common children had figurines dressed in the clothes of the common people.

AN AMAZING FIND!

In 1999, archaeologists began work at a site in Túpac Amaru, Peru, to save hundreds of mummy bundles from destruction. The mummy bundles, like Egyptian mummies, included **mummified** (preserved) bodies, but the cloth wrappings also included many other special items.

Scientists have found as many as seven people in one bundle. The bodies have been well preserved because of the exceptionally dry climate. Many still have their eyes! Within the bundles, archaeologists have also found many personal items, including sandals, guinea pigs that had been sacrificed and placed in the bundle, gourds, corn, potatoes, macaw feathers, and warrior clubs.

Many of the mummy bundles have "false heads," a cloth bag of cotton that has been attached to the bundle to represent a head and make the mummy bundle look more human. Some of the heads have wigs and masks, but no facial features. This type of burial, bundling the dead in layers of textiles, is typical of pre-Inca and Inca burials. The upper class bundled their deceased in fine textiles. Kings' bodies were preserved, most likely with a variety of herbs, and were kept in the palace. Because kings were thought to be divine beings, they were never considered to be really dead.

RELIGION

Inca religion centered around the belief in and worship of many gods. The people believed that it was important to lead a good life, following all religious practices, in order to insure the goodwill of the gods. When a person experienced adversity, whether physical or personal, they believed it was a punishment for wrongdoing.

Major Gods

The Inca worshiped six major gods.

Viracocha, the Creator, was believed to be both mother and father of the Moon and the Sun. The Inca believed that Viracocha also created Thunder, the Stars, the Earth, and the Sea. Man was believed to be created in Viracocha's image.

Inti, the Sun god, was believed to be a divine ancestor of the Inca. The Sun was in charge of all of the other gods. Important temples were built throughout the empire to honor the Sun. Inti's golden image was kept in the most important temple in Cuzco, the Temple of the Sun, also called the *Coricancha,* which means "golden enclosure." Contained within its golden walls were images of gods, fountains, **altars** (raised structures where prayers or sacrifices are offered in worship), a miniature corn garden, hummingbirds, lizards, life-size llamas, and masks, all made of solid gold.

Ilyap'a, the Weather or Thunder god, was believed to be the messenger of the Sun. When rain was needed, the Inca prayed to this god. The Inca believed that when the rain finally fell, Ilyap'a had broken the rain jug. Many shrines were built to honor him.

Mama-Quilla, Mother Moon, represented the king's wife, the *Coya.* This goddess had a separate shrine from her husband, the Sun, and her shrine was managed by priestesses. The stars were believed to be the children of the Sun and the Moon.

Pacha-mama, the Mother Earth goddess, was connected to agriculture. The Inca placed a large stone in the fields to represent Pacha-mama. She watched over and protected the fields.

Mama-cocha, the Water goddess, was associated with the sea, the lakes, and the highland waters. The coastal fisherman worshiped this goddess.

These gods were responsible for important events that effected Inca life, especially farming. Without the earth, sun, and rain, the Inca could not farm. Without the sea, people living on the coast would not have food. There were other gods below these gods, but they were less important and were not represented by any images. Only the Creator and the Sun and Weather gods were represented by images.

Religion centered around worship of the Sun god, Inti. The Inca held religious ceremonies to honor Inti in the holiest of all temples, the Temple of the Sun, which was located in the center of Cuzco.

Sacred Places

The Inca considered certain places or objects to be sacred. These might be mountains, caves, bodies of water, rocks, temples, hills, bridges, houses, battlefields, or other things in the natural world. The Inca called these sacred places or objects **huacas.** The Inca believed that spirits resided at the huacas, and they often conducted sacrifices, rituals, or ceremonies at these sacred places. The Inca also had amulets, or charms, that they believed had supernatural powers. These charms served as portable huacas because they could be carried around.

Priests and Priestesses

The high priest held this position for life and lived in Cuzco. He was in charge of all priests and priestesses and the temples and shrines throughout the empire. Some priests ran the temples and shrines and others worked to serve and assist the high priest. Priests performed many duties, including hearing confessions, giving penance, **divining** (foretelling future events), praying, performing sacrifices, explaining the gods' desires to the people, performing religious ceremonies, and diagnosing and treating illnesses.

Priestesses sometimes had the same jobs at temples as priests. However, most priestesses were responsible for honoring and serving the shrine to the Moon. They were expected to carry the Moon's silver image with them.

A Time to Pray

Praying and showing reverence to the gods were important parts of daily life. People prayed out loud, silently, or by making gestures. One such gesture, called *mocha,* was made by bowing from the waist with the arms stretched above the head. While bowing, people brought their hands to their lips and kissed their fingertips. Traditional, more formal prayers were said by priests during important public ceremonies, but most of the people could recite a simple standard prayer or make one up as they worked. The people were given prayers to say after confession. However, if the priest suspected that they were not being honest about their sins, he tested his suspicions by divination. If it was determined that a person had not told the truth, the person received the punishment of having a large stone dropped on his or her back. The Inca nobles confessed only in private directly to the Sun.

Beautiful young girls around ten years old were selected from villages throughout the empire to become the Chosen Women. Noble young girls were also selected. These young women, called *Acllas* (virgins), were brought to the provincial capitals where they lived in special houses for their training by the *Mamacunas,* nuns or Consecrated Women who devoted their lives to teaching. They learned weaving, household duties, and religion. After their training, which took three to five years, the girls were brought to Cuzco to be presented to the king. He selected the best and most beautiful to serve him and become his wives. Many of those not selected to be wives were given to high-ranking curacas as additional wives. Some were kept for special sacrifices, while others stayed at the temple to train other girls who would be chosen. The high priestess was responsible for the well-being of all the Chosen Women.

Sacrifices

The Inca king and the priests conducted sacrifices on a number of occasions, including during religious ceremonies and public feasts, when honoring the gods, or in times of difficulty. Animals, such as llamas, guinea pigs, and birds, usually were offered as sacrifices. But cloth was also offered as a sacrifice to the gods. At the king's coronation or in times of stress, such as famine, war, or the king's illness, humans might be sacrificed. Some ritual sacrifices took place high in the mountains. The person being sacrificed may have been given medicinal herbs to induce sleep. The victim was wrapped in a wool mantle, given some personal items, then left to freeze to death.

A daily sacrifice to the Sun was conducted in the main square of Cuzco. A wood fire was lit just before the Sun rose. Food prepared especially for this sacrifice was thrown into the fire for the Sun to eat. Another special sacrifice happened at the beginning of each month. The king and the noble officials gathered together and dedicated 100 llamas to the Creator. The llamas were divided among the participants and each, in turn, gave their llamas to be sacrificed during the course of the month.

THE GOLDEN IMAGE OF INTI

The largest and most important image of Inti was made of solid gold and hung in the Temple of the Sun in Cuzco. The Spanish described the image as being "of great size

and made of gold." The image, as large as a man, was disc-shaped and had rays projecting from its face. Other images of Inti, located in Sun temples throughout the empire, were also made of gold but were smaller in size.

Most gold objects were made from thin sheets that were cut to the desired shape or hammered over a wooden form. To create a face on the object, the back of the metal sheet was hammered onto the form, which produced a **relief** (raised part of a surface) design on the face. The image of Inti may have been created using this technique. You will create your image from clay.

the clay if you like, as shown here. In case you'd like to hang your Inti in your room, you can also poke a hole in the top of the face using the tip of the paintbrush handle. Let the clay harden according to the directions that came with the clay.

Cut out sections of the outer edge.

Press the modeling tool into the clay to create the face, but don't go through the clay.

- self- or air-hardening clay
- small bowl of water
- modeling tool
- paintbrush
- gold acrylic craft paint
- paper towels for spills and cleanup

STEPS

1 Flatten a ball of clay into a pancake with a thickness of about $1/2$ inch (1 cm) and a diameter of about 7 inches (18 cm). Smooth all cracks and lines using your fingers.

2 Use the modeling tool to carve a face on Inti. Don't cut through the clay, just press down enough to create an impression. Carve a design around the outside edge of

3 After the clay has hardened, paint the front gold, let it dry, then paint the back gold and let it dry completely.

Each day at sunrise and sunset, Inca priests sang *jaillis*, or sacred hymns. These jaillis were prayers and thoughts about the gods. The Inca considered jaillis to be the highest form of poetry, which the Inca enjoyed. Even the common people sang farming jaillis as they worked together in the fields.

FOOD

Some of the most common dishes prepared by the Inca were a variety of soups and stews from the many crops they grew, such as potatoes, corn, beans, squash, tomatoes, chili peppers, and quinoa. Sometimes meat was also included. These hearty dishes were often served as the main morning meal.

Corn

Corn, or maize, grew in the warmer areas at lower altitudes of the Inca empire, and was an important food source. The Inca ate corn almost daily, either boiled, roasted, or ground to make flour. On special occasions, they used the corn flour to make maize cakes or **tamales** (cornmeal dough rolled with ground meat or beans, seasoned with chili, wrapped in corn husks, and steamed). Maize porridge, called *capia*, was a favorite. The Inca liked a kind of roasted corn called *cancha*, which they considered a delicacy. Today we know this food as popcorn.

PASS THE GOURD, PLEASE

The Inca even made a beer, called *chicha,* from corn. Everyone drank chicha. The working class drank it from gourds or clay vessels. The upper class and nobles drank chicha from silver or gold cups, called *qero.*

Potatoes

Potatoes originated in the Andes and have been cultivated there for almost 10,000 years. This important food was a major part of the Inca diet, mainly because it grew well at high altitudes. The Inca grew more than 150 varieties of potatoes in many sizes, shapes, and colors. A few varieties even survived in subzero temperatures!

The Spanish brought the potato to Europe, where it was cultivated and spread to other parts of the world, including North America.

Quinoa

Quinoa (KEEN-wah), a hearty grain that grows at high elevations very near the snow line, was a staple for the Inca for many years. The Inca made cereal and flour from quinoa, and they also used it to thicken soups and stews. Quinoa is a complete protein food, which means it does not need to be eaten with any meat. Quinoa also blends well with other foods. Every year at the start of the planting season, the king broke the ground using a gold spade and planted the first quinoa seed. This grain was so important to the Inca that they called it *chisiya mama,* which means "mother grain."

HOT STUFF!

Hot chili peppers, or *uchu,* both dried and fresh, were used to season most dishes and were a favorite ingredient in stews.

FREEZE-DRIED FOOD

The Inca wanted to eat potatoes year-round, so they invented a food preservation method called **dehydration** (the process of removing water from food). In the evening, farmers wet the potatoes with water and left them out overnight to freeze, which caused their skins to crack. The next day the potatoes were left in the hot sun to dry completely. As the skins became brittle, the farmers shuffled around the cracked and dried potatoes with their feet until the skins completely fell off, leaving a lightweight, dried potato that could be stored for a long time. When the potatoes were needed for food, the cook simply added water and the potatoes were ready for cooking.

Meat

Meat was usually eaten on special occasions. Llama meat was also eaten, but only rarely, since the llama was such an important animal and had many other uses. The only readily available meat was from guinea pigs, which the Inca raised. The Inca enjoyed this meat roasted and mixed with other ingredients in stew. Dried meat, prepared much like dried potatoes, was more available than fresh meat. To dry the meat, the Inca exposed strips of meat to freezing temperatures at night and hot, dry temperatures during the next day. Then the strips were pounded between two stones, which made the meat very thin and dried out even further. Dried meat could be stored for a long time.

The king feasted on fresh meat whenever he pleased. Runners also brought him a variety of fresh fish from the coast.

∽◊∽ ANDEAN STEW ∽◊∽

Stews and soups were so popular because boiling food was an easy and efficient method to prepare dishes for a large family. Many foods could be cooked together to create a hearty dish. One favorite of the upper class, called *locro,* was made with dried and fresh meat, chili peppers, potatoes, and corn. Another stew, called *montepatasca,* included corn, chili

peppers, and herbs. When quinoa was added to thicken this stew, the Inca called this dish *pisqui.* The Inca used salt as a seasoning for most foods.

This recipe, which is based on Inca stew, contains many of the foods the Inca used in their stews. *Note: Ask an adult for help before using the knife and the stove.*

INGREDIENTS

SERVINGS: 4

- 2 potatoes
- water
- 1 14.5-ounce (411-g) can of stewed tomatoes
- 1 15-ounce (432-g) can of corn
- 1 7-ounce (198-g) can of mild chopped chili peppers
- 1 14.5-ounce (411-g) can of chicken broth
- $\frac{1}{8}$ to $\frac{1}{4}$ teaspoon (.5 to 1 ml) ground chili pepper (optional)
- salt and pepper to taste

UTENSILS

- potato peeler
- cutting board
- sharp knife
- 1 large saucepan
- can opener
- large colander
- 1 long-handled cooking spoon
- measuring spoons
- serving bowls

STEPS

1 Peel the potatoes, then cut them into medium-size chunks. Place the potatoes in the large saucepan. Add enough water to cover the potatoes. Bring the water to a boil over high heat. As soon as the water boils, turn the heat down to medium-high and cook the potatoes until they are partially cooked, about 10 minutes. *Ask an adult* to help you drain the potatoes into the large colander. Place the potatoes back in the large saucepan.

2 Open the can of stewed tomatoes, but do not drain off the liquid. Pour the tomatoes and the liquid into the large saucepan with the potatoes.

3 Open the can of corn, drain off the water, then empty the corn into the large saucepan. Repeat this step for the can of chili peppers.

4 Open the can of chicken broth and add the broth to the large saucepan.

5 Stir until all the ingredients are mixed together. To make a spicier stew, add the ground chili pepper and stir. Bring the stew to a boil, then cook on medium heat for about 5 minutes, stirring occasionally.

6 Serve the stew immediately in the serving bowls and add salt and pepper if you like.

AN ANCIENT FACT!

Spondylus (a type of oyster) shells have been found in mummy bundles. The Inca believed that the gods would eat the oysters as an offering.

QUINOA SNACK

Here's a simple recipe for making quinoa as a snack.

INGREDIENTS

SERVINGS: 2

- 1 cup (240 ml) of quinoa (available at health food stores and some super-markets)
- 2 cups (480 ml) water
- milk
- brown sugar to taste

UTENSILS

- measuring cup
- fine mesh strainer
- medium saucepan with cover
- serving bowls

---

1   Measure the quinoa, put it in the strainer, and rinse it under running water. Put the quinoa into the saucepan. Add the water. Bring to a boil over high heat. As soon as the water boils, turn the heat down to low, cover the pot, and cook the quinoa for 15 to 20 minutes.

2   Serve the quinoa in the bowls, then pour in a little milk, and add a little brown sugar to taste.

REFRIGERATION WITHOUT ELECTRICITY

In order to keep their drinks cool, the Inca stored beverages in large ceramic pots that they buried halfway into the ground.

CLOTHING

Clothes for both common people and the upper classes were simple. The basic outfit for women included a long sleeveless dress that was pinned at the shoulders, a long mantle worn over the dress, and a sash tied around the waist. When a woman went outdoors, she wore a shoulder mantle held together with a metal pin called a *topu.* Noble women used topus made of gold or silver, while lower-class women had bronze or copper topus. Some women in present-day Peru and Bolivia continue to use this traditional accessory.

AN ANCIENT FACT!

Some topus had large discs at the top that served as mirrors.

A man wore a loincloth, which was a long piece of cloth that was wrapped around the waist and between the legs. He also wore a **tunic** (a slip-on garment made with or without sleeves, usually knee-length or longer, and sometimes belted at the waist), called an *uncu,* over the loincloth. Cloaks were worn over the shoulders when the weather got chilly. Men and women both carried small purses or pouches under their cloaks to hold amulets, good luck charms, and coca leaves, which they chewed. A noble's pouch might be sewn with gold and silver thread or decorated with feathers and tiny plates of silver and gold.

Children wore the same types of clothes as adults. Finely woven, child-sized tunics have been found in ancient graves.

FOR THE FEET

Both men and women wore similar types of sandals. The soles of the sandals were often made from the neck of a llama. The Inca upper-class people wore sandals made from the fibers of the aloe plant, wool, straw, cloth, and leather from the llama. Sandals worn by nobles, especially during ceremonies, were decorated with tiny gold and silver masks. The lower classes rarely wore shoes, but when they did, the sandals were simply made, with no decoration.

Cotton and Wool

The Inca used a variety of materials to make their clothes. People who lived on the coast mostly used cotton, which grew abundantly there. The highland Inca preferred wool and sometimes a combination of cotton and wool. Most wool came from the alpaca, while wool for the nobles' garments came from the vicuña. Vicuña wool had a much softer, silkier feel.

Designs

The woven or embroidered designs on Inca clothing ranged from simple to elaborate. Geometric designs, shapes used in repeating patterns, were popular, as were symbols that represented things from the natural world, myths, and ancient traditions. Designs called *tocapus* were placed across the waist of a tunic and stood for the wearer's status, or rank in society and also for his or her place of origin.

All people in the empire wore the same types of clothing, but there were noticable differences. The lower classes added little color or design to the natural-colored cotton and alpaca fibers. However, the king and upper-class people wore brightly colored, more elaborately decorated clothes. Clothing dyes were created using **indigo** (a blue dye made from indigo plants) and **cochineal** (a red dye made from the dried body of the cochineal insect), and the bark of the false pepper tree may have been used to make a yellow color. Minerals were also used as dyes.

INCA TUNIC

One unique feature of Inca clothes, and especially tunics, was the amount and type of design on the tunic. The most important design used was geometric. Small squares, usually arranged in rows, decorated the tunic. The higher up the wearer was on the social ladder, the more geometric designs there were on the tunic. A ruler might have a tunic covered in rows of squares with the squares containing recurring designs. A ruler might also have inverted triangles around the neck of his tunic. The head of the army would wear a tunic with more designs than his soldiers, who wore distinctive designs depending on their rank. It is believed that these designs had specific meanings, but there is no information about what the meanings might be.

In this activity, you will make a simple Inca tunic from a white pillowcase, then decorate it with your own geometric design pattern based on Inca designs.

SUPPLIES

- 1 white pillowcase (choose standard, queen, or king size depending on your body size)
- pencil
- scissors
- masking tape
- a few paper shopping bags
- fabric paint in a variety of colors (this can be found in craft or discount stores) or permanent markers in a variety of colors, if you can't find fabric paint

- paintbrush (if using paint)
- small bowl of water (if using paint)
- paper towels (if using paint)

STEPS

1   If you use a new pillowcase, first wash and dry it. Use the pencil to lightly draw a curved line along the top, sewn edge of the pillow case. Cut along the curve. This is the opening for your head. Draw two curves on the sides of the pillowcase for armholes, then cut along these lines.

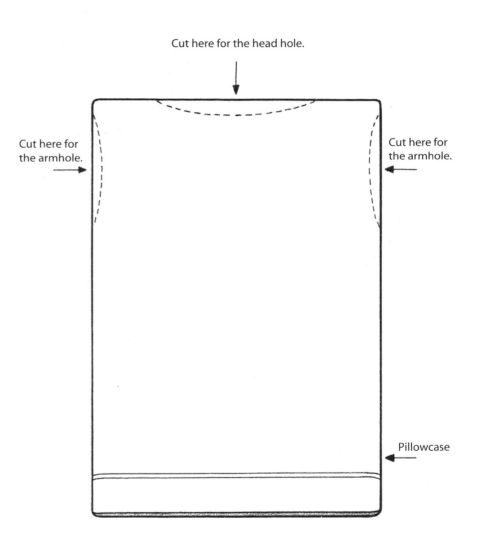

Cut here for the head hole.

Cut here for the armhole.

Cut here for the armhole.

Pillowcase

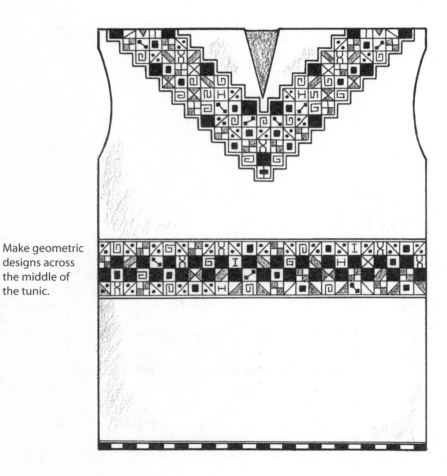

2   Tape the shoulder and side edges of the pillowcase to your work surface. Slide the shopping bags inside the pillowcase so the paint or markers won't seep through to the back of the pillowcase. Decide how many designs your tunic will have and how much of the tunic will be covered with designs. You might want to have geometric designs only around the waist area, from the neck down to the bottom edge, or over the entire surface. Use the pencil to lightly draw some Inca designs, such as the ones shown here, on the front of the pillowcase.

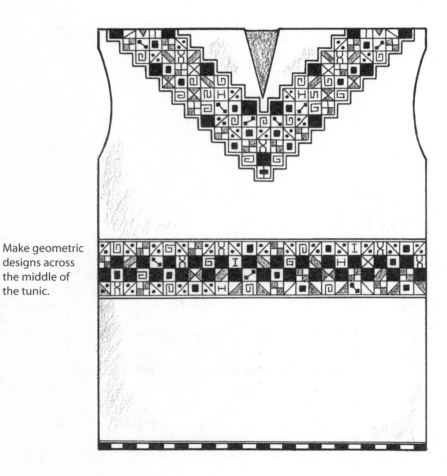

Make more geometric designs on the tunic.

Make geometric designs across the middle of the tunic.

Place the paper bag inside of the pillow case.

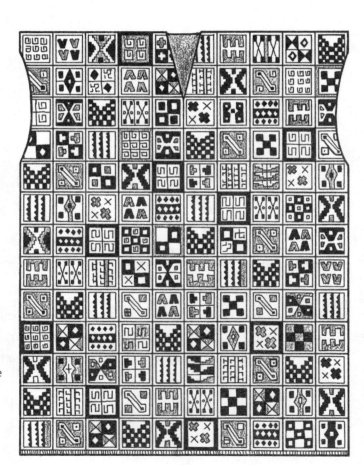

3 After you have finished drawing your designs, either paint them using the fabric paint or color them in using the markers. After you finish sections of the pillowcase, lift the front side of the pillowcase away from the bags so it doesn't stick and dry to the bags. Do this occasionally as you work. When you are finished, let the paint or marker ink dry.

4 Decorate the back of the pillowcase as you did for the front and let the paint or marker ink dry completely.

PART THREE

ARTS

Language arts, including oral plays, poetry, myths, folk tales, and legends, played an important role in Inca life. Plays could be comedies or dramas. Actors were often from the upper class. The Inca were also keen visual artists who excelled in the arts of pottery, weaving, metalworking, jewelry making, woodworking, and stonecutting. Much of the decorative art the Inca created had geometric designs with intricate and complex patterns. Inca nobility wore tunics that were carefully woven with such designs and patterns. These same designs were also used as a decorative element on pottery pieces designed for the upper class, including cups, bowls, and plates.

The artisans who created these pieces lived in the capital cities and in Cuzco because they created beautiful works of art for the upper class and the royal family. They worked full-time at their craft and did not have to pay taxes in the form of other work. They were supported by the families they worked for and were given all the supplies they needed to create their works of art. Parents taught their children these special skills so they would carry on these traditions.

PLAYS AND POETRY

Plays were performed by members of the upper class for the king and his court on special occasions. Plays were created orally, then repeated by the performer until he or she had completely memorized the words. A good performance was rewarded with gifts of gold and jewelry. Both dramas and comedies were performed. Dramas focused on the war heroes and the great kings of the past. Comedies were about family life, agriculture, and household themes. Sometimes dance or drum and flute music accompanied a play.

Poetry

Because the Inca did not have a written language, all of their stories, songs, and poetry were passed down orally from generation to generation. At the time of the conquest, some love poems, dramas, narrative poems, and hymns were written down by the Spanish.

Poets carefully constructed their poetry and occasionally ended lines with rhyming words. However, most of the poetry was written in blank verse, which is poetry written in unrhymed lines. Love was an important theme for these poems, but nostalgia was also a popular theme.

Narrative poems were usually recited or sung in the open plaza for special occasions. Most of these narratives were about the king and his accomplishments. When a king was not a strong leader or had not achieved much, narratives were not written about him. This may have been the case with Inca Urcon, who was Pachacuti's brother. When he became king, he failed to protect Cuzco from the invading Chanca army. Pachacuti immediately stepped in and took over, saving Cuzco from the Chanca. Much narrative poetry about Pachacuti exists, but little was apparently created about his brother. Here's an example of one verse from a narrative poem about the death of Pachacuti Inca:

I was born like a lily in the garden,
And so also was I brought up.
As my age came, I have grown up,
And, as I had to die, so I dried up,
  And I died.

WRITE A POEM

Try writing your own poem. It can be a narrative poem, which tells a story or explains an important event in your life. Or you can try to write in blank verse, which does not have to rhyme. Since many of the Inca poems were about the kings' lives, why not write a poem about your life? It can be as long or as short as you like. All you need to get started is paper, a pencil, and your creative thoughts.

Here's an example of a blank verse:

VIOLIN
by Jill Decker

> *I love to play the violin*
> *Bringing music to my ears.*
> *My hand flies across the fingerboard,*
> *Music filling the air.*

WEAVING

All Inca women, including the most elite, wove cloth. It gave women great pride to weave and make clothes. Some men were also expected to weave for the government, but they wove things like ropes and mats. Weaving took up more time than any other task or craft and, after farming, was the most important industry in the empire. Weavers from the coastal areas used cotton, and highland weavers preferred wool. Wool provided extra warmth for those living at the higher elevations. Llamas, alpacas, and vicuñas grazed the highlands and were herded for their wool. Archaeologists believe that one reason the Inca developed weaving into such a high art form was because they had domesticated these animals, which provided the wool. The domestication of these animals was unique to the Inca.

Weavers created elaborate designs using a simple backstrap loom. This loom consisted of two wooden bars onto which the yarn was attached. A strap, which the weaver wore around his or her back, was attached to the bottom bar. The top bar was attached to a tree. The weaver could adjust the tension of the weaving by moving his or her body forward or backward. This simple method of weaving could be done almost anywhere.

Llamas, alpacas, and vicuñas produced wool in a variety of shades of brown, black, and white. This gave weavers many natural color options when weaving. The Inca graded the wool according to its quality. The finest wool came from the vicuña and was used for making clothes for the nobles. Alpaca wool came next and was used for the bulk of weaving. The Inca used the coarse wool from the llama for weaving pouches, cords, and mats.

Spinning on the Go

Because weaving was such an important part of a woman's life, she often spun fibers whenever she had an opportunity. One popular time was while walking to the market. The weaver would position a stick containing clumps of cotton or wool fibers under her arm. From the clump, the woman would pull some loose fibers, which she attached to a wooden

spindle that was weighted at one end. Holding the fiber strand, she let the spindle hang down and twirled it as she walked. The spinning motion spun the fibers into thread. Back at home, the woman stored this spun thread and all her sewing and weaving supplies in a reed workbasket. These baskets have been found in Inca graves. It is believed they were meant to accompany the women to the afterlife so they could continue weaving.

The Inca are known for their exceptional textile weaving. Historians speculate that the Inca excelled in this art because of the plentiful wool and because their advanced farming techniques enabled them to spend less time in the fields and devote more time to weaving. Inca fabrics were very tightly woven. As a comparison, modern weaving may have about 60 cross-threads per inch. Some of the ancient textiles found have as many as 500 cross-threads per inch!

An Eye for Design

Inca weavers created beautiful designs as they wove. The most popular were abstract geometric designs using squares, oblongs, and rectangles. To add additional decorative elements, the weaver often included images of humans, animals, fish, birds, and gods. Often the weaver wove these designs into the textile itself. They also used a technique called *embroidery*. The design was stitched directly on the finished woven textile, giving the design a slightly raised appearance. At burial sites in the dry coastal areas, archaeologists have

THE IMPORTANCE OF CLOTH

Woven cloth was one of the most important items made by the Inca. It had many uses in Inca society. A woven garment helped to identify where a person was from. This was important, since it made keeping track of people easier. A person who tried to leave his or her province would be recognized quickly because of his or her clothes.

Specific colors and designs woven into the cloth indicated status in society. Royals, of course, wore clothes made from the most exquisite cloth, called *cumbi*. Cumbi cloth, made from vicuña wool, was dyed in the most vibrant colors. Gold and silver threads and tropical bird feathers added decoration and texture to the outfit.

Cloth played a major role in ceremonial rituals. Because they sacrificed things of value, the Inca burned cloth as an offering to the gods at most sacrifices. According to some accounts, during one period the Inca burned as many as one hundred finely woven cloths every morning as an offering to the Sun god.

Cloth was also given as a gift to a conquered leader. The victor gave the cloth as a sign of respect, and the leader accepted the cloth as a sign that his people would become part of the Inca empire. Soldiers also received cloth as payment for their services.

found some well-preserved textiles and ceremonial robes that have exquisitely embroidered designs.

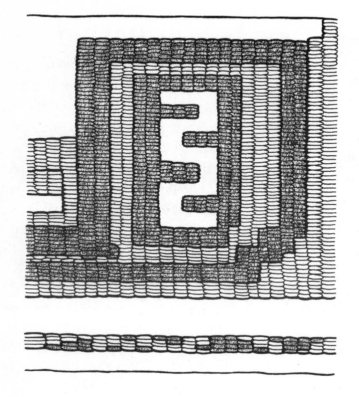

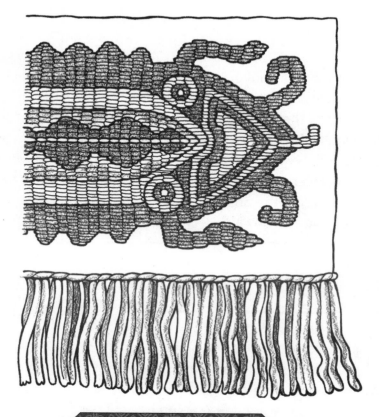

WOVEN LLAMA DESIGN

Images of llamas, as well as alpacas and vicuñas, were often depicted in the Inca's woven cloth. In this activity, you will create a woven llama design as the Inca did.

SUPPLIES

- 1 piece of heavy cardboard, 5½ by 3 inches (14 by 8 cm)
- ruler
- pencil
- scissors
- cotton yarn, any color
- acrylic or wool yarn in a variety of colors
- embroidery needle with blunt tip

STEPS

1 Along each long edge of the cardboard rectangle, make 21 pencil marks ¹/₄ inch (.5 cm) apart.

2 Cut on the marks to make slits about ¹/₄ inch (.5 cm) deep. This cardboard piece is your loom.

3 Use the pencil to lightly draw a llama in the center of the loom. When you are pleased with your drawing, go over the lines to darken them.

4 Cut a piece of cotton yarn about 4 yards (3.5 m) long. This piece of yarn is going to become the **warp** (stationary strands on a loom). Place the warp on the loom by putting it through the bottom left slit, leaving a 10-inch

Draw the llama in the center of the cardboard.

5¹/₂ inches (14 cm)

3 inches (8 cm)

Draw both ears as one.

Draw the front legs as one and the back legs as one.

Cut slits ¹/₄ inch (.5 cm) apart and ¹/₄ inch (.5 cm) deep on each long side.

(25-cm) tail out the back of the loom. Wrap the yarn around the loom, working from bottom to top and left to right through each slit in turn. When you reach the top right slit, leave a 10-inch (25-cm) tail out the back of the loom. Turn the loom over and tie the two tails together in a tight knot.

5 Cut a piece of acrylic or wool yarn in any color about 60 inches (152 cm) long and thread it through the needle.

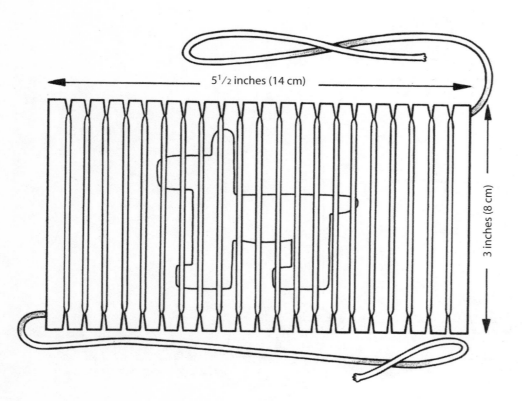

5¹/₂ inches (14 cm)

3 inches (8 cm)

This piece of yarn is a the **weft** (a strand that is woven into the warp).

6 Turn the loom faceup and start weaving at the bottom right of the loom by placing the needle *under* the first warp, then *over* the next warp, *under* the next, and so on until you reach the left side of the loom. Gently pull the weft all the way through, leaving a 4-inch (10-cm) tail on the right. For the second row, weave back toward the right side of the loom, placing the needle *over* the first left warp, *under* the next warp, and so on until you reach the right side. Tug the weft gently, making sure the left and right sides of the warp don't pull in. Use your fingers to pack, or push down, each row close to the previous one. *Do this each time you weave a row.*

◀▦▦▧ **WEAVING TIP** ▨▦▦▶

When you need a new color, start weaving the new color on the opposite side of where you just ended. Remember to weave the new row opposite of the way you wove the previous row. Do not cut the yarn ends that are sticking out. You will cut these later. Make sure the yarn ends are about 2 inches (5 cm) long.

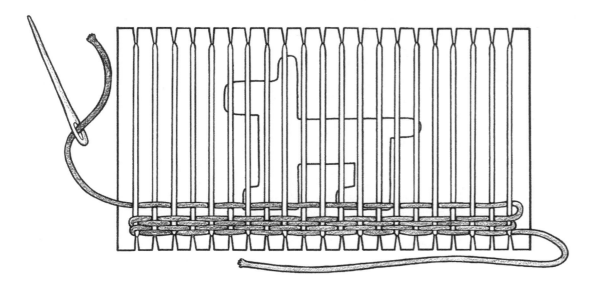

7 Continue weaving until the rows reach the bottom of the llama's feet. End that row. Now you will begin to weave the llama. Choose a color for the llama, then start weaving at the bottom of the back feet. Weave up the back legs, across the body, across the head, and up the ears, then end the weaving. Next weave the front feet and legs, then end that weaving.

Weave over the outline of the llama starting with the back legs. Weave across the body, the head, the ears, and then across the front legs. Use a new piece of yarn for the front legs.

End the row at the base of the llama's feet.

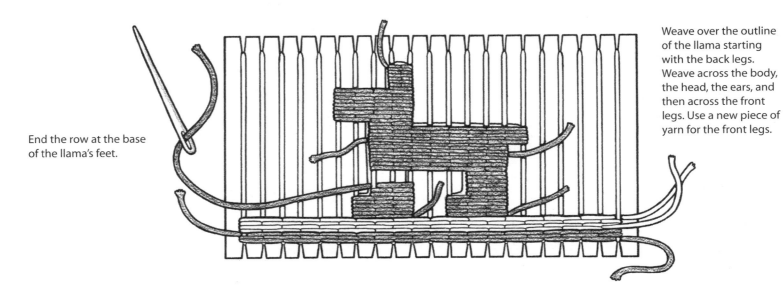

8 Next weave the space in between the llama's legs with the same color yarn you used for the background. When you get to the llama's legs, you will need to bring the needle around the warp the legs are woven on, as shown.

9 Continue weaving to fill in the space on the right side of the llama, then on the left. As you approach the outside edge of the legs on both sides, remember to bring the needle around the weft the legs are woven on. Finish weaving until you reach the top of the loom. If it gets too difficult to weave near the top because there is less open space on the loom, you can stop before you reach the top.

10 Turn the loom facedown and cut across the middle of the unwoven warp, cutting through the two knotted strands.

11 Turn the loom faceup and remove the warp strands from the slits along the bottom of the cardboard. Tie the first two warp strands on the bottom left together

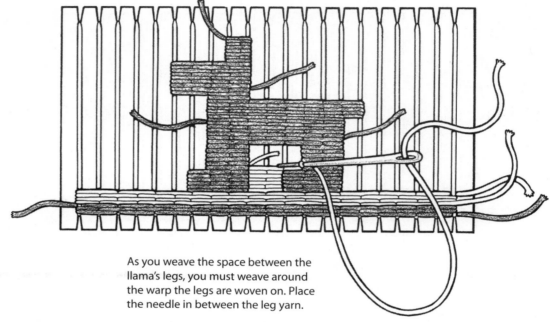

As you weave the space between the llama's legs, you must weave around the warp the legs are woven on. Place the needle in between the leg yarn.

in a tight knot close to the edge of the weaving. Tie the next pair of strands together and so on until all pairs are tied. Both weft tails should be tied in a knot to the nearest warp strand.

12 Repeat step 11 for the warp strands at the top of the weaving.

13 Trim the warp strands to a length of about ¼ inch (.5 cm).

14 Carefully trim from the weft the yarn ends that are sticking out of the rows.

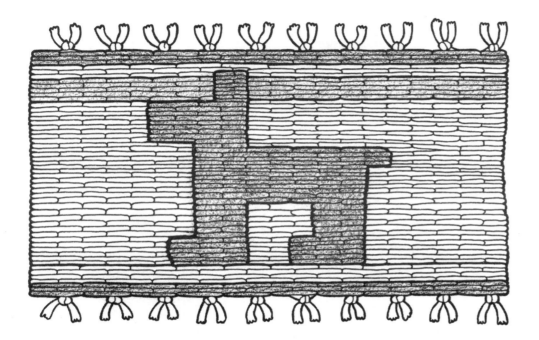

The llama was domesticated thousands of years before the Inca gained power. Llamas can live in very cold temperatures as well as in desert heat. These animals were used for carrying loads, not people. If a person tried to ride a llama, this stubborn animal would stop and sit down in place. The descendants of the Inca continue to raise and herd llamas and rely on this animal to carry loads to and from town.

POTTERY

The Inca were skilled potters and created useful as well as decorative pieces. They made dishes and cups, storage containers, cooking pots, and carrying containers. Many plates had a handle in the shape of an animal head, such as a bird, duck, or puma. Jugs and jars were often crafted in the shape of humans or vegetables. Images of corncobs were popular on many jugs. The traditional Inca jug called the *arybola* was used to hold liquids such as chicha. The jug had a rope attached to it and was carried on a person's back. This type of jug is still made today by the Inca descendants.

Cuzco was the center for pottery production, although it was produced throughout the empire. All pottery was created by hand using a coil method. Coils of clay were placed on top of each other to build the piece into a specific shape. The coils were then smoothed with the fingers or sometimes with stones, and the piece was painted with designs.

Some designs were incised, or scratched into the surface. After the pot dried, the potter polished it using a stone, then fired it in an open fire.

Pottery Designs

The Inca used geometric designs on their pottery in repetitive patterns. Designs included squares, triangles, diamonds, and lines. The designer often combined a variety of designs to create different effects, such as a checkerboard pattern using a lot of small squares. Stylized images of animals, including pumas, jaguars, llamas, lizards, frogs, and birds, were also used to decorate pottery. However, cooking pots had little or no painted designs. One of the few designs found on cookware were stylized clay snakes that had been attached to the outside of the pots.

AN AMAZING FIND!

In 1999, the well-preserved bodies of three Inca children were found on Mount Llullaillaco located on the border of Chile and Argentina. Many items were found with the children, who had probably been left there as a sacrifice. Some items included pottery storage containers that still had food in them! The stored food was probably left so that the children would have food for their journey to the afterlife.

PORTRAIT JUG

The Inca potters crafted jugs and vases in the shape of the head of a special person, such as a warrior, a king, or a god. These pieces became known as portrait pottery. In this activity, you will make your own clay portrait jug.

SUPPLIES

- self- or water-hardening clay
- small bowl of water
- modeling tool
- paintbrush
- acrylic paint in a variety of colors

CLAY COIL TIP

To make a coil, roll a piece of clay between your hands until it is about 8 to 10 inches (20 to 25 cm) long with a thickness of about 1/2 inch (1.5 cm). Tear off any excess clay from the coil after laying the coil on the clay base. Repeat this trimming step for each coil after you place it on top of the coil below.

STEPS

1 Mold a piece of clay into a flat pancake that measures 3 inches (8 cm) across and has a thickness of 1/4 inch (.5 cm). Smooth all lines and cracks with moist fingers. This piece forms the bottom of the jug.

2 Make your jug by placing clay coils, one on top of the other, to build the sides. After each coil is in position, gently blend the seams together, as shown.

Blend the coil with the jug, inside and out.

3 As you build the jug, use your fingers to carefully push out the middle area of the jug to form a head shape. Push out from the inside of the jug. As you add coils to the middle and top of the jug, make the coils shorter and shorter so that the top of the head curves in. At the very top, leave an opening so the inside of the jug can harden. Gently push in the bottom front sides to form a chin.

Leave a hole at the top.

Press the middle section out, working from the inside of the jug.

Press in here on both sides to form chin.

4 Add the facial features. Mold the nose in the shape of a solid triangle, **score** (mark with lines or scratches) the back of the nose and the area of the face where it will be attached, moisten these surfaces, and press the nose on.

To score a surface, use the pointed end of your modeling tool, to make a few lines on flat surfaces that will touch. Then rub a little water on these surfaces before pressing them together. This will help "cement" the surfaces to each other.

Smooth the nose edges into the face and add shape to the nose. For the eyes and mouth, roll the clay into very thin strips, then score and moisten the surfaces that will touch and place them on the face. Gently press them into the face, but keep the shape of these parts. Next add ears. Finally, add hair or a hat. Use the modeling tool to add definition to the ears or other parts of the face. Smooth all lines and cracks with a moist finger. Let the jug head harden according to the directions that came with the clay.

5 Paint your portrait jug any colors you like. Let the paint dry completely.

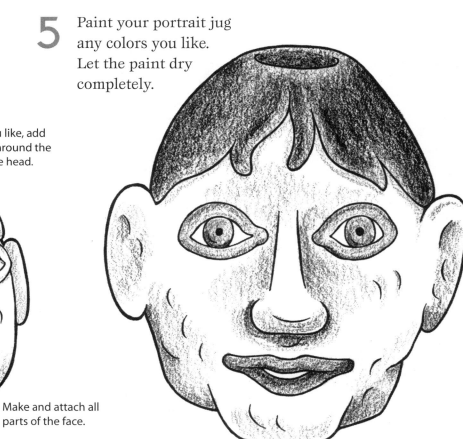

If you like, add hair around the entire head.

Make and attach all parts of the face.

METALWORKING

The Inca and other Andean cultures excelled in the art of metalworking. Some of the oldest pieces of metalwork, including tools, found in the region date back 3,500 years. Early forms of the art were crude, with little decoration. But by the time the Inca were dominant in the Andes, metalworking had developed into a more elaborate art, and the Inca were creating many magnificent pieces, including masks, figurines, jewelry, and life-sized animal figures.

Valuable Objects

The Inca used gold, silver, copper, and tin to create drinking cups, plates, jars, bowls, jugs, jewelry, animal figurines, masks, and statues. Objects made from gold and silver were reserved for the king and the nobles. The lower classes used copper to make objects such as shawl pins, decorations for clothing, and knives. Metalworkers often combined two of these metals together to make an object. Objects that were **inlaid** (set into the surface of a material to create a design) with precious stones, such as turquoise, were highly prized. After a person of status died, many gold and silver objects were buried with the body.

Mining Techniques

The information about Inca mining comes from Spanish chroniclers' accounts and from what archaeologists have found. The Inca mines appear to have been like caves. A worker would dig an opening in the earth just large enough for him to fit in. He would use deer antlers or pointed stones to dig out pieces of earth, which were then placed in llama-hide sacks. Doing this helped to enlarge the cave, as well as remove the **ore** (mineral containing a valuable metal) that was in the dirt. The worker carried the sack of earth out of the mine to where other workers would separate the metal from the dirt. As the cave became larger, the inside became too dark for the worker to move about. At this point, the miner dug another cave.

Miners also found gold grains or gold dust in mountain rivers and streams. The Inca used shallow pans to scoop up gravel from the streambed, then washed the gravel to make the gold easier to pick out. Gold nuggets were large enough to simply be collected. Removing metals embedded in rock required **smelting** (the process of melting at high temperatures to separate metal from rock).

Because mining required hard physical labor, miners worked only from noon to sundown in the summer to help prevent exhaustion. All lower-class households were required to send one person to work in the mines for a certain period of time each year.

WIND FURNACE

To smelt metals, the Inca used wind furnaces called *huairas*. These terra-cotta, cylinder-shaped furnaces had a series of holes on the sides. A pile of adobe bricks mixed with charcoal was placed inside the furnace. The furnaces were placed on hillsides so the wind could blow through the openings, fueling the fire that had been ignited inside. The metal-embedded rocks were placed inside, and as the furnace heated up, the metals melted and collected in containers at the bottom of the furnaces.

Working the Metal

Inca metalworkers used a variety of techniques to craft the metal into beautiful objects. Casting was used to make a mold of an animal or other object. Hot, melted metal was poured into the mold and then left to harden. The mold was removed, revealing the metal in the shape of the animal. Casting was used mostly for metals other than gold and silver. Most tools, such as ax blades and knives, were made using this method.

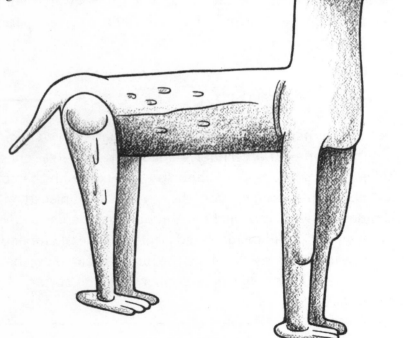

The hammering method seems to have been used for silver and gold. The Inca used stone hammers to pound gold and silver into thin sheets that were then used to make various objects. For intricate design work, the Inca used inlaying, which involved setting tiny pieces of precious stones into the metal. The Spaniards raved about the incredible beauty of the objects with inlaid designs. Some objects were sent to Spain as gifts to the king. Most pieces, however, were melted down, making it easier to store and ship the metal to Spain, so very few examples of Inca metalwork remain.

SILVER LLAMA

A silver llama figurine was unearthed in 1996 from the ruins of a sacrificial site on Mt. Sarasara some 18,070 feet (5,508 m) above sea level. Found in a bundle of textiles, the llama was in perfect condition, without a single trace of tarnish! Most of the silver and gold llamas were made from hammered sheets of metal that were bent into body shapes. Then the metalworker had to **solder** (join metallic surfaces by using an alloy, such as tin, that served as a bonding substance) the separate body pieces together. In this activity, you will create a llama in aluminum foil similar to the ones the Inca metalworkers made from sheets of silver.

SUPPLIES

- 1 sheet of paper, 8½ by 11 inches (22 by 28 cm)
- pencil
- scissors
- 1 sheet of art embossing aluminum, 8 by 12 inches (20 by 30 cm), available at craft stores
- paintbrush
- liquid glue

STEPS

1 With the pencil, draw a llama shape like the one shown here on the white paper. The llama should measure approximately 6 inches (15 cm) from the tip of the ear to the bottom of the foot and 5 inches (13 cm) from the tip of the nose to the tip of the tail. Then cut it out with the scissors. This is your template.

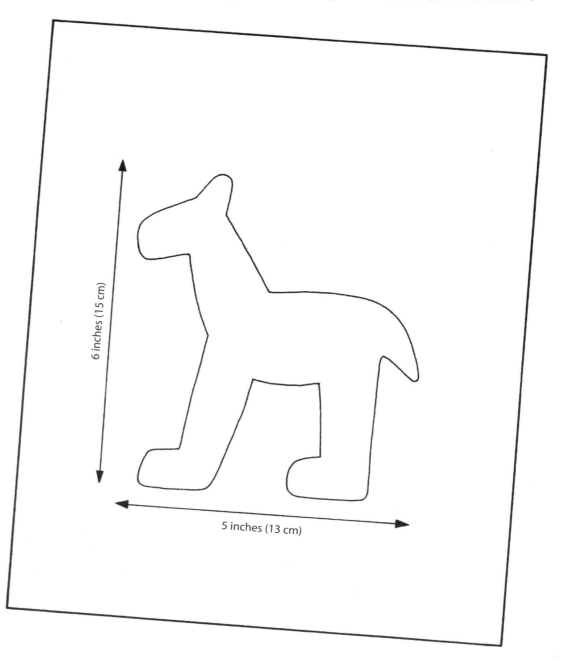

6 inches (15 cm)

5 inches (13 cm)

2 Fold the aluminum sheet in half along the 8-inch (20 cm) edge so it measures 8 inches (20 cm) by 6 inches (15 cm). Place the paper llama template on the aluminum sheet with the tip of the ear on the fold. Hold the template in place while you trace around it on the aluminum using the rounded tip of the paintbrush.

3 Remove the paper llama. Cut out the aluminum llama through both layers of the aluminum, but leave the llama connected at the rounded tip of the ear at the fold in the aluminum. Open the llama and lay it flat on your work surface. Place small drops of glue inside the llama bottom half, being careful not to glue the feet and lower leg area.

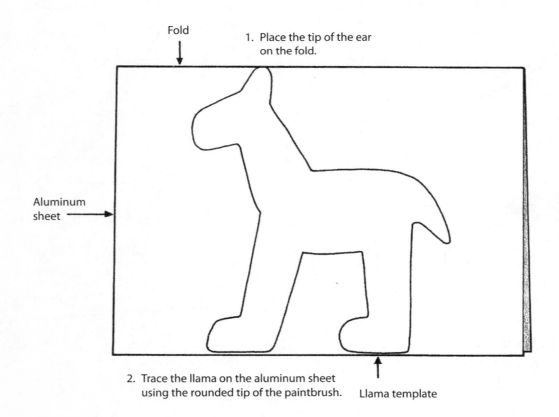

Fold

1. Place the tip of the ear on the fold.

Aluminum sheet

2. Trace the llama on the aluminum sheet using the rounded tip of the paintbrush.

Llama template

4 Fold down the top half over the glued half so both pieces of the llama line up. Press the llama halves together gently. Let the glue dry completely.

5 Use the rounded tip of the paintbrush to incise, or carve, details onto one side of the llama. Use enough pressure so that the design shows through on the other side. Carve an eye, mouth, nose, and lines for hair on the neck, body, tail, and legs.

6 Gently separate the unglued part of the feet and legs so your llama will stand.

AN ANCIENT FACT!

The Inca called gold "sweat of the sun" and silver "tears of the moon."

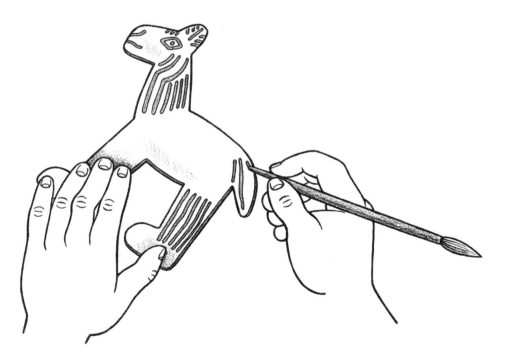

ACHIEVEMENTS

Although the Inca had no written language or written numerals, they devised a unique tracking network, using knotted cords, that gave a complete picture of the important information that was needed to run the empire. The king relied on this system to know what was going on anywhere in his empire at any time.

The Inca also excelled in engineering and stoneworking. With simple tools, they created massive stone structures and walls that didn't need mortar to be held together. The stones were carved so expertly that each one fit perfectly with the next. Many of these structures are still standing today. One of the most imposing examples of Inca architecture still stands high above the city of Cuzco. The massive walls of this fortress, known as Sacsahuaman, create a zigzag pattern that must have intimidated the most aggressive invaders. Some of the stone blocks in this structure weigh as much as 100 tons! Thousands of Inca worked on Sacsahuaman, and experts believe it took almost 30 years to complete. This fortress may also have been a holy place, because temple ruins have been found inside the walls.

RECORD KEEPING

To keep track of all the important details of the empire, the Inca invented an ingenious method using knots on a string. They called these knotted strings *quipus* (KEE-poos). Royal *quipucamayocs* were specially trained to create and interpret the knots to keep track of everything from crop production and the amount of food in storage to the number of births, deaths, and weapons in the empire. Varying knots and yarn color represented different information. Quipus were not used to count individual items but instead recorded totals. The counting process was done using grains or pebbles. Many quipus were destroyed by the Spanish conquerors because to them the quipus represented a practice followed by **pagans** (people whose religion involves many gods). Today, no one knows for sure what information was represented by which knots.

Long-Distance Messengers

In such a large empire, getting messages to all parts of the empire was challenging. But the Inca met this challenge by using runners called *chasquis* to deliver messages. Runners either carried quipus with them or simply relayed a verbal message. Way stations, buildings where runners could rest and wait for their turn to run the next part of a message relay, had been set up throughout the empire. These way stations were about 8 to 15 miles (13 to 24 km) apart. As the runner approached the station, he blew a conch shell trumpet to announce his arrival. Hearing the sound, the next runner came out to meet the chasqui, took the quipu from him, and began his run, losing no time. In this way, a group of runners could cover 250 miles a day.

AN ANCIENT FACT!

The Inca understood the concept of zero as meaning nothing. Only two other ancient civilizations used zero—the Hindi of what is now India and the Maya of what is now Guatemala, Mexico, Belize, Honduras, and Costa Rica.

Grouping by Tens

The Inca used a **decimal system** (base 10) of counting. They also used this system to organize households and even individuals in the empire. Everyone, including workers and supervisors, was placed into groups of 10. Here's how it worked: Ten workers made up one group and reported to a boss. The second group of 10 reported to another boss. The third group of 10 did the same, and so on. The 10 bosses who supervised each group of 10 workers reported to another boss. For households, it worked the same way. Each group of 10 households was supervised by a curaca. Ten curaca were managed by another curaca, and so on.

Color Combinations

The quipu maker used a variety of colors for each quipu, and it is believed that the colors were significant to the information recorded. Red, yellow, blue, green, and natural shades were the most common. But the quipu maker was able to get many variations with these basic colors by combining or twisting strings together to make a new string. For example, by twisting two solid colors, such as red and yellow, the quipu maker created a candy cane effect. This would be considered a new color. By twisting two colors in the opposite direction, the quipu maker created a totally different effect and a new color. Or two colors could be joined together so that one color was at one end and the other color at the opposite end. All of the single colors could be combined to create many different color combinations.

QUIPU

Quipus consisted of a main cord or string from which many other primary strings hung. Secondary strings could be hung from the primary strings. If needed, strings could also be hung from the secondary strings. A quipu might have a main string with only a few primary cords, or it might have hundreds of primary and secondary strings. Each type of knot and its position on one of the hanging strings represented specific information. In addition to numerical information, the quipus also recorded laws and historical information.

We don't know exactly what the Inca knots meant, but you can learn how to make a few of the different Inca knots and use them to keep track of something you want to remember.

SUPPLIES

◆ string, medium thickness
◆ ruler
◆ scissors

STEPS

1 Cut a piece of string about 12 inches (30 cm) long. Cut 2 more pieces of string, each about 24 inches (61 cm) long. Tie each 24-inch (61 cm) piece to the 12-inch (30 cm) piece, as shown.

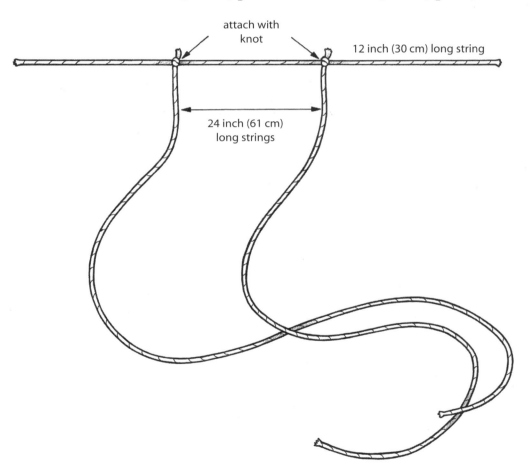

attach with knot

12 inch (30 cm) long string

24 inch (61 cm) long strings

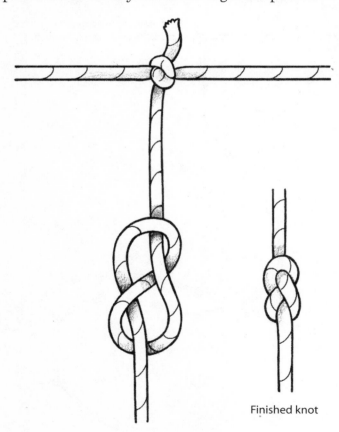

2 Now you will learn to tie two simple knots, using the 24-inch (61 cm) strings. The first knot is a figure eight. Hold the left string in your left hand. Take the end of the string in your right hand. Bring it under the upper part of the string, then around the upper part of the string, then behind and down through the loop. Gently pull the end until you see the eight-shaped knot.

Finished knot

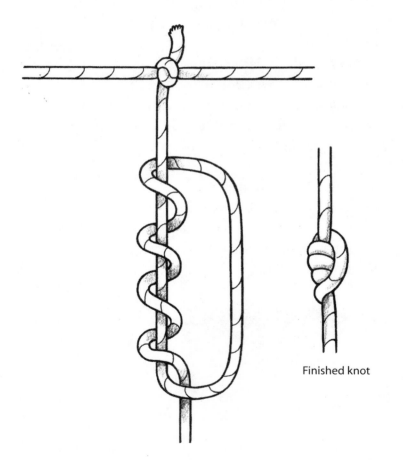

3 The next knot is a long knot. Use the string on the right. With your right hand, bring the end of the string under the upper part of the string, then wrap it around the string three times. Finally, insert the end of the string down into the loop. Gently pull the knot together until it is tight.

Finished knot

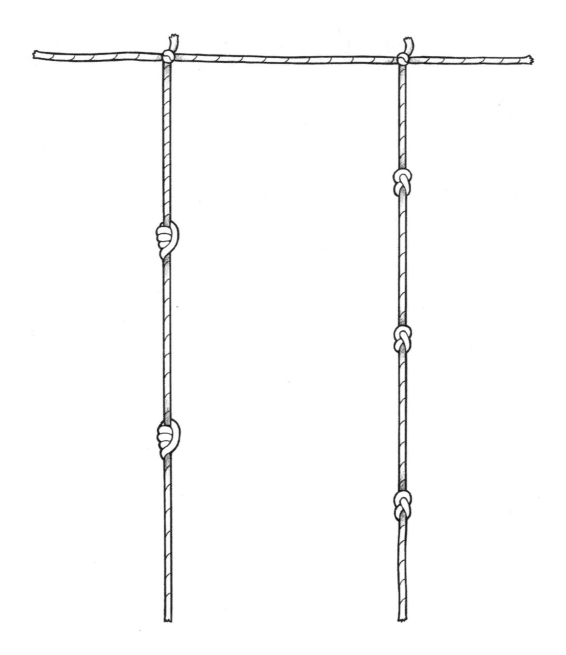

MASTER BUILDERS

The Inca were highly skilled stoneworkers and constructed roads and buildings using massive stones that they cut by hand. They chiseled these stones so precisely that after they were fit together even the thinnest of objects, such as a knife blade, would not fit between them. The only thing keeping these stones together was their precise fit. No cement or mortar was ever used. These ancient structures have survived earthquakes!

Roads

The Inca built a highly sophisticated road system that was paved with flat stones and clay bricks. This elaborate network of roads spread throughout the empire and helped link people in the mountain and desert regions with Cuzco, the capital. The entire road system spanned nearly 12,000 miles (20,000 km). The roads were built over all types of terrain. In swampy areas, the Inca built up sections of earth to support the roads. Along the coast, the Inca used sun-baked clay to make roads. Narrow roads of stone were built into the sides of mountains. For royal use only, the Inca constructed two roads that ran the length of the empire. One was in the highlands, and the other was near the coast.

The Inca also constructed houses or inns along the roads so that people making long journeys could rest. Stone pillars were set up along the way to mark distances, similar to mileage signs used on present-day roads.

Bridges

To cross rivers and deep gorges, the Inca built suspension bridges. They constructed these bridges from aloe and maguey plant fibers, which were woven into long, thick strands of rope, some as long as 400 to 500 feet (122 to 152 m). The floor of a bridge was made with sticks and more fibers attached by the rope strands. The Inca attached the ends of the rope strands to stone posts on either side of the

river or gorge. These bridges proved to be quite strong, but for safety reasons, Inca workers replaced the ropes every year. The Spanish explorer Francisco Pizarro and his men, who had to cross many of these bridges, were often terrified by the experience. Highland Indians who live in remote villages continue to make and use these bridges today.

Stonecutting

The stones for Inca walls, buildings, and roads were cut using nothing more than stone and bronze hammers, axes, and chisels. The stonecutter had a difficult and time-consuming job because he had to grind or pound the edges of the stone until it fit perfectly with the stones surrounding it. He then polished each stone using sand and another stone. Unskilled workers most likely helped the stonecutter to quarry the stone, move it by tying rope around it and dragging it, and place it in position after the stonecutter had finished his work.

MACHU PICCHU

Machu Picchu, called the lost city of the Inca because it was never found by the Spanish, is located high above the Urubamba River in the Andes Mountains. An American archeologist, Hiram Bingham, discovered the city in 1911. Machu Picchu may have been a royal estate or a religious retreat that was built sometime around A.D. 1450 by the Inca ruler Pachacuti. Machu Picchu, which means "manly peak," is noted for its incredible architecture and stonework. All of its structures, including homes, warehouses, and temples, blend with the rugged terrain and seem to fit naturally with the surroundings. One of the most impressive buildings is the Sun Temple, especially its perfectly curved wall. It is believed that more than 1,000 people, most likely relatives of Pachacuti, lived in Machu Picchu at its height.

STONE WALL

Many stone walls had a jigsaw look, with different-sized cut stones fitting together perfectly. Some stones had as many as twelve cut sides. The Inca usually reserved this jigsaw design for stone walls. Precisely cut stones of the same size were used for the more important buildings, including temples, the king's home, and administrative buildings.

In this activity, you'll build a stone wall from clay blocks using Inca techniques to create a jigsaw design.

SUPPLIES

- self- or water-hardening clay
- modeling tool
- small bowl of water
- acrylic paint
- paintbrush
- paper towels

STEPS

1 Make different-shaped clay blocks for the bottom row of your wall. The blocks should measure at least $^1/_2$ inch (1.5 cm) wide and between $^3/_4$ to $1^1/_2$ inches (2 cm to 4 cm) long. Make enough blocks to form a wall about 7 inches (18 cm) long. Before placing the blocks next to one another to make the bottom row, score (see page 65) the surfaces that will touch and then wet the scored surfaces using the paintbrush.

2 Gently press the two scored surfaces together. *Don't smooth the line between the two surfaces.* You want to see this line. After pressing the blocks together, adjust the shape of the block with your fingers if necessary.

AN AMAZING FIND!

Although many of the Inca buildings were made from stone, adobe bricks were used as well. One of the largest surviving Inca temples along the coast of Peru is made of more than 140 million adobe bricks!

3 Continue building the wall by making clay blocks of different shapes, scoring the edges, and gently pressing the blocks together until you have three or four rows. You can place two flat pieces of clay under the wall at the two sides for support, as shown in the illustration below. Let the wall harden completely according to the directions that came with the clay.

4 Paint your wall in colors that resemble those of an Inca wall, such as tan, gray, and brown. You might use one color, then use the others to add contrast.

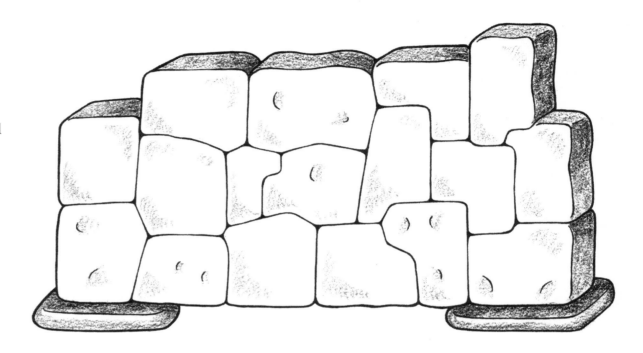

ENTERTAINMENT

Although the Inca worked hard every day, they did find time for fun. Festivals were held for agricultural activities, the coronation of a new king, or a victory at war. The type of festival generally determined how the people celebrated. During many, including *Chacra Cona* and *Hatun Cuzqui*, sacrifices to the huacas played a major role, especially llama sacrifice. During the *Inti Raymi* festival, the royal family sang to the sacred llama, a pure white llama that symbolized the first llama on earth. Feasting and drinking chicha, dancing in the public plaza, and singing were part of many festivals.

KEY FESTIVALS

 few ceremonies stood out as more important than any others.

Inti Raymi, or Feast of the Sun, was held in June to honor the Sun god, Inti. The Inca celebrated Inti Raymi near Cuzco, and only royal Inca and nobles could attend. During the festival, the participants sacrificed 100 llamas. They carved statues in wood and dressed them in fine woven cloth, then burned them to honor Inti and Viracocha. After the sacrifices had been completed, the bones from the llamas were buried on a nearby hill. Then the festival continued for days, with music and dancing. Today the descendants of the Inca continue to celebrate this important time of year.

Coya Rami, the Feast of the Moon, was celebrated in September. The men had the job of cleansing the city of sickness by conducting rituals to drive away illness. Then everyone bathed and smeared maize porridge above the doorways of their houses as a sign of their purification. The people feasted and danced for days after this festival.

Capac Raymi, the Magnificent Festival, was held in December to celebrate the rainy season. This festival included the summer solstice, the longest day of the year. To mark the beginning of this festival, all nonresidents of Cuzco had to leave the town. They had to stay away until the festival ended three weeks later. During this festival, the male coming-of-age ritual was completed and ceremonies honoring several gods were held.

Aymoray Quilla, the Great Cultivation, was held in May to celebrated the corn harvest. As corn was brought from the fields, everyone danced, sang, and asked the gods for enough corn to last until the next harvest. Llamas were sacrificed, and the meat was distributed to all the Inca. Some meat was burned at all the huacas in Cuzco.

MUSIC

The Inca created beautiful music for their festivals using a variety of musical instruments. One of the most popular instruments was the *quena,* a flute made from a piece of cane that was open at both ends and had several finger holes along the top side. Flutes were also made from clay, animal bones, and wood. Whistles made from clay and wood were popular, but these could produce only one note. The *pototo* was like a trumpet and was made from a large **conch** (seashell). It made a loud sound that could be heard from far away and was mainly used during times of war. Drums were made from animal skins stretched over a base of wood or clay. Some were used in wartime. Others were used for religious ceremonies or special occasions and had fancy gold and silver decorations. Bells, shaken with the hand or worn around the ankle during dances, were made from copper, bronze, and silver. The Inca made rattles from snail shells, deer hoofs, animal bones, clay, and seashells filled with dried beans.

Haunting Sound of the Andes

The **panpipe** (a wind instrument made of short pipes of varying lengths that are bound together in a vertical row) has been played in the Andean region for a long time, but it was the Inca who perfected this instrument. The Inca made their panpipes from hollow reeds, clay, quills, and bones. The hollow pipes were cut into different lengths, arranged in order from longest to shortest, then held together with quills and yarn. The player would hold the instrument so the pipes were vertical and blow over the top holes to produce different sounds. Sometimes the instrument had two tiers of pipes. The Inca often carved designs into their panpipes or attached feathers to them.

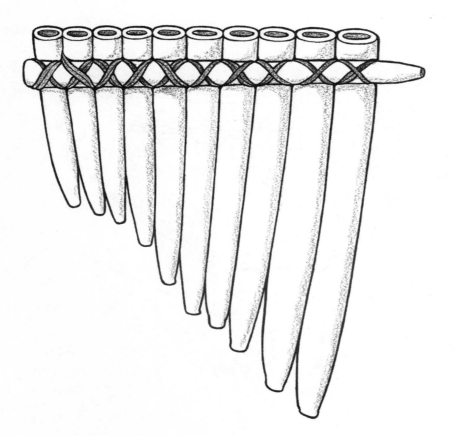

PANPIPE

Try your hand at making your own panpipe from clay.

SUPPLIES

- self- or water-hardening clay
- 1 dowel with a diameter of $\frac{1}{4}$ inch (.5 cm)
- liquid glue
- moist paper towels
- duct tape

STEPS

1 Make 8 hollow clay tubes following the instructions in step 2. The first pipe should be 8 inches (20 cm), and

each one after that should decrease in size by $^1/_2$ inch (1.5 cm). The last tube should measure $4^1/_2$ inches (11.5 cm).

2 To make each tube, roll a piece of clay until it is the right length and about $^3/_4$ of an inch (2 cm) thick. Hold the piece of clay in one hand while you carefully push the dowel into the center of one end of the clay tube. Push the dowel through the length of the clay tube, gently rotating the dowel as you push. Stop just before it reaches the opposite end of the clay tube. You want that end to remain closed to make a tight seal. Try not to poke a hole through the sides of the tube. If you do, repair it with additional clay. Make sure the opening in the tube is uniform. To do this, rotate the dowel in the tube a few times.

3 After all the clay tubes are hollow, measure them again to make sure they are the correct sizes. Make adjustments, if needed, by slicing off clay at the open end for clay tubes that are too long, or adding a little clay at the open end for clay tubes that are too short. Lightly tap both ends of each clay tube on your work surface to flatten them. Adjust the open end to make sure it has a nice round opening.

4 Smooth all lines and cracks in the tubes with moist fingers. Let the tubes harden according to the directions that came with the clay.

5 You will need to glue the tubes together. Lay the tubes in a row from longest to shortest, lining them up at the open ends. Move the tubes apart so they don't touch. Leave the longest tube on your work surface. Pick up

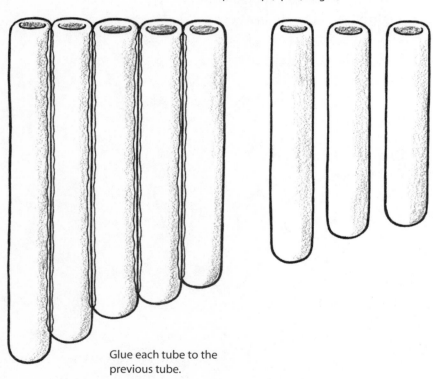

the next tube in line, squeeze a line of glue along its length, then gently place it against the longest tube and hold it there for a minute. Take the next tube in line, squeeze a line of glue along its length, and then place it against the tube you just glued. Hold it in place for a minute.

Line up the top (open) edges.

Glue each tube to the previous tube.

6 Continue gluing the remaining tubes to each other following the directions in step 5. Let the glue dry completely. Use moist paper towels to wipe any glue that drips on the tubes.

7 Place a piece of duct tape around the tubes as shown in the illustration below. This will help hold the panpipe together. To play your panpipe, hold the open end level with your mouth and gently blow across the holes.

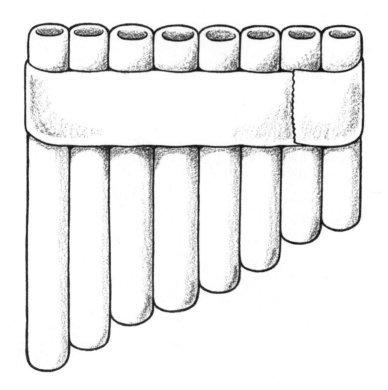

DANCE

Dance was an important part of most festivals and public religious ceremonies. In Cuzco, dancers wore elaborate costumes and performed specific dance steps that they had practiced beforehand. Within the provinces, dancers' costumes and dance routines varied. They did not have to follow the more formal approach used in Cuzco.

Each ceremony had its own special dance. Farmers danced the *haylyc* when they conducted the planting ritual. The *cachua* was performed for warriors going off to battle. Dancers formed a circle, holding hands with one another while dancing. The *huay-yaya* was danced only by royal family members.

Dance Instruments

In addition to wearing costumes for dancing, the Inca often danced with shakers or bells attached to their bodies. These shakers made noise as a person danced. Different parts of the empire had unique traditions for their music and dance, including which instruments were played or used in dancing. In Cuzco, copper bells and animal hoofs were used as shakers and were fastened at the knees and ankles. The bells were shaped like cones or small spheres and had a stone or tiny metal ball inside. In the jungle region east of Cuzco, the Antis people also wore shakers, but these shakers were fastened at the knees and hung down to the ankles on strings. The shakers moved about freely as the person danced.

DANCE BELLS

It is easy to make a pair of Inca–style dance bells using bells and yarn.

STEPS

1 Wrap a piece of yarn 3 times around the top of your calf, just under your knee. Cut the yarn at that length.

Then cut 5 more pieces of assorted colors of yarn to the same length as the one you already measured. You will use these pieces to make 2 yarn braids, with 3 pieces of yarn per braid.

2 To braid the yarn, hold three strands of different colored yarn together and tie one end in a tight knot. Tape the knotted end to your work space. Separate the three strands. Place the left strand over the middle strand, then place the right strand over the new middle strand. Repeat by placing the new left strand over the new middle, then the new right strand over the new middle. (See page 15 for more on braiding yarn.)

3 Follow this braiding pattern until you have about 3 inches (8 cm) of unbraided yarn left. Tie this end in a tight knot. Make the second yarn braid using the remaining cut yarn pieces.

4 Cut between 22 and 26 yarn strands about 6 to 7 inches long (15 to 18 cm) in different colors. Separate the strands into two equal groups. Now tie one braid around the top of each of your calves in a small bow. Tie the short yarn strands to each braid by pushing one end of each strand between the braid and your leg. Knot that end of the strand around the braid. Don't tie any strands where you tied the braid in a bow. Try to tie the strands so that they hang at slightly different lengths.

5 Take the braids off your legs and attach a bell to the other end of each yarn strand. If you can't push the yarn through the hole at the top of the bell, use a piece of embroidery floss to attach the bell. Tie the floss to the bell and then tie the floss to the yarn.

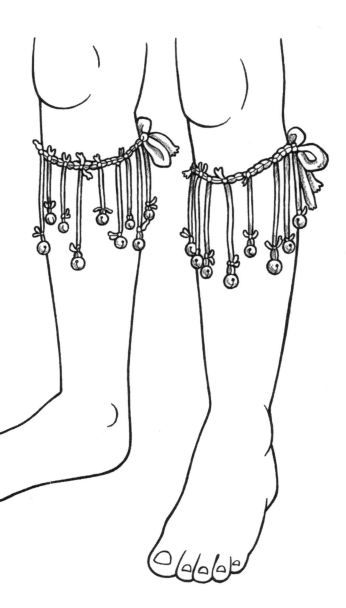

GAMES

Not much is known about the games the Inca played. Playtime was not generally encouraged because Inca society emphasized organized work for all people in the empire. Children were expected to help their parents in these work efforts. However, children did amuse themselves with balls made from animal hides and played a game called *papa auqui,* which means potato chief. Unfortunately, little is known about how this game was played.

Adults played some games using dice that had five marks on them and were made from clay or wood. It is thought that the dice were thrown to determine how many moves a game piece, such as dried beans or broken pottery pieces, could be advanced. Carved stones have been found that may have been used as game boards. The Inca may have also played a game that involved holding a seed pod between two fingers and shooting it to see who could get it to go the farthest distance.

Legend has it that Pizarro found out about a game Atahuallpa enjoyed playing in the 1500s. He had Atahuallpa teach him how to play, then Pizarro brought the game to Spain so people there could play. Pizarro called it *Perudo,* but to the

GAMES OF SKILL

Upper-class boys participated in games of skill designed to help them prepare for warfare. They competed in races and staged mock battles. Although these games were fun, they were also serious, and participants could be injured.

Inca it was known as the "bluffing game" because players bid and bluffed their way through it. Atahuallpa may have used a game board similar to the one shown here.

GUESSING GAME

Now you and your friends can play a much easier version of the game Atahuallpa played. But instead of bluffing, you'll be guessing.

- 1 sheet of paper
- pencil
- 6 or more six-sided dice, depending on the number of players
- 2 or more plastic cups, depending on the number of players

Object of the Game: The first person to get 50 points wins.

Number of Players: 2 or more

Game Rules

1 One player writes each person's name on the sheet of paper to keep track of the scores.

2 Players take 1 plastic cup and 3 dice each. Players place their dice in their cups, shake the cups, then turn the cups upside down on the table. Keep the cups over the dice to hide them from the other players. Players do not look at their dice, either.

3 Each player guesses the total number of dots on his or her own faceup dice. Everyone tells their guesses. Then players look at their own dice and count the dots on the sides facing up. The player who comes closest to his or her guess wins a point, which the scorekeeper records

under that person's score name. The game continues until someone gets 50 points.

(Note: The highest number anyone can get is 18 if all three dice have the sixes faceup. The lowest number anyone can get is 3 if all three dice show the ones faceup.)

TOYS

Simple toys, such as a top called *pisqoynyo,* were used by children. Possibly made from animal bones or clay, the top had a long piece of yarn wrapped around it. When the child tugged the yarn, the top whipped free and spun around on its pointed end. In some pre-Columbian graves in what is now southern Peru, archaeologists have found miniature balsa rafts with attached sails. Experts believe that the rafts may have been toys because of their size and the fact that they have been found in children's graves.

Balsa Wood

Balsa trees grow in the humid rain forests and coastal areas of Central and South America. The word *balsa* is a Spanish word that means "raft." The wood is lightweight and floats well, and the Inca used it to make large rafts as long as 20 feet (6.1 m). These rafts had two poles attached at one end to form an inverted V, to which sails were fastened. The Inca used these balsa rafts for coastal fishing.

Legend or Fact

There are a number of sources that tell of Topa Yupanqui, the tenth Inca ruler and son of Pacha-cuti, sailing on a balsa raft in the late 1400s from the coast of what is now present day Ecuador to two islands, Ninachumbi, which means "island of fire," and Avachumbi, which means "island beyond." Topa Yupanqui had heard stories about these islands from traders and decided to make the journey. He sailed with a full fleet of balsa rafts and 20,000 men in search of the islands. It is said he returned a year later. There are also reports from the Spanish that Inca scholars talked about migrations the Inca took on balsa rafts, possibly to the South Pacific.

～ BALSA RAFT ～

With this activity, you will make a toy balsa raft that actually floats!

SUPPLIES

- 5 pieces of balsa, 1 inch by 6 inches (2.5 by 15 cm)
- 6 pieces of balsa, 1 inch by 5 inches (2.5 by 13 cm)
- liquid glue
- paper towels
- pencil
- 1 piece of paper, 8½ by 6 inches (22 by 15 cm)
- 1 dowel, ¼ inch by 8 inches (.5 by 20 cm)
- small ball of self-hardening clay

STEPS

1 Lay the 6-inch (15-cm) pieces of balsa side by side on your work surface. Drizzle some glue over the surface of the wood.

2 Lay the 5-inch (13-cm) pieces of balsa over the 6-inch (15-cm) pieces, placing them in the opposite direction, as shown.

3 After all the pieces are in place, gently press them together. If any glue squeezes out, use a damp paper towel to wipe it off. Lift up the

Line up the bottom slats one next to another.

Drizzle the glue over the surface of the bottom slats.

raft to wipe off with the paper towels any glue that has come out of the bottom. Set the raft aside to let the glue dry completely.

4 Use the pencil to poke two holes in the 8½-by-6-inch (22-by-15-cm) piece of paper. Poke the first hole ½ inch (1 cm) down from the top short edge of the paper, centering the hole horizontally. Poke the second hole

½ inch (1.5 cm) up from the bottom short edge of the paper in the center. The second hole should also be centered horizontally and should line up with the first hole. This is the sail.

5 Gently push the dowel through the two holes in the sail. Adjust the paper to make it puff out on one side. Squeeze glue on the raft surface about ⅓ of the way

down from the top short edge. Place the small ball of clay on top of the glue and press it into place. Stick the dowel into the clay, smoothing the clay around the base of the dowel. Let the clay harden. If the clay has cracked after it is dry, rub liquid glue all around the base of the clay and over its surface. Let this glue dry completely. Now your raft is ready to set sail.

KON TIKI

In 1947, Thor Heyerdahl, a modern-day Norwegian explorer, built a balsa raft patterned after the Inca rafts and set out from Peru on a voyage across the Pacific Ocean. He called his boat *Kon-Tiki*. After 101 days, he landed on the Polynesian island of Raroia in the South Pacific, approximately 4,000 miles (6,400 km) from his starting point. He suggested that the Inca may have used balsa rafts to voyage out into the Pacific, making their way to Polynesia as well as other places, such as Easter Island.

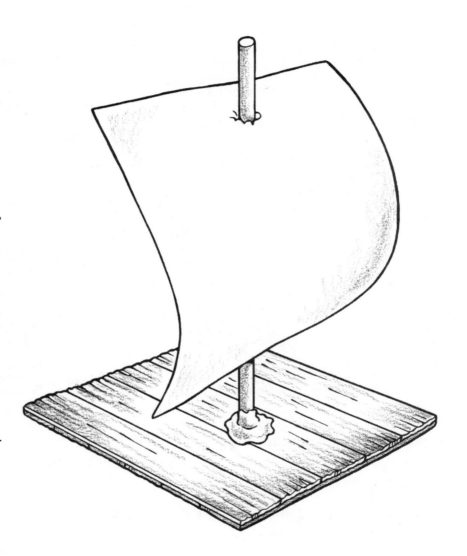

GLOSSARY

adobe   A brick or building material made of sun-dried earth and straw.

altar   A raised structure where prayers or sacrifices are offered in worship.

archaeology   The scientific study of material remains, such as fossil relics, artifacts, and monuments of past human life and activities.

canal   Artificial waterway used for draining or irrigating land.

coat of arms   An identifying crest or emblem.

cochineal   A red dye made from the dried body of the cochineal insect.

conch   A seashell.

conquistador   Someone who conquers.

decimal system   Base 10 system of counting.

dehydration   The process of removing water from food.

divination   The practice of foretelling future events.

huaca   Inca sacred place or structure.

indigo   A blue dye made from indigo plants.

inlaid   Set into the surface of a material to create a design.

litter   A chair with poles attached, used for carrying important people.

mortar   A mixture of cement, lime, sand, and water that hardens and is used as a plaster.

mummified   Preserved.

ore   Mineral containing a valuable metal.

pagan   A person whose religion involves many gods.

panpipes   Wind instrument made of short pipes of varying lengths that are bound together in a vertical row.

quinoa   An Andes region plant whose seeds are ground and used as food.

quipu   A method of record keeping using knotted strings.

relief   Raised part of a surface.

score   To mark with lines or scratches.

smelting   The process of melting at high temperatures to separate metal from rock.

solder   To join metallic surfaces by using an alloy, such as tin, that serves as a bonding substance.

spondylus   A type of oyster.

tamales   Cornmeal dough rolled with ground meat or beans, seasoned with chili, wrapped in corn husks, and steamed.

thatch   Any type of plant material used as a cover.

tuber   A fleshy edible root crop.

tunic   A slip-on garment made with or without sleeves, usually knee-length or longer, and sometimes belted at the waist

warp   The stationary strands on a loom.

weft   A strand that is woven into the warp.

INDEX

gold *(continued)*
    as "sweat of the sun," 71
    in *topus,* 42
government officials, 3, 7
grains, 3, 28, 37, 38, 41
Great Cultivation, 89
Guaman Poma de Ayala,
    Felipe, 1
guava, 1
guessing game activity, 99–100
guinea pigs, 30, 33, 39

H hammering method, for metal-
    working, 68
Hanac-paca, 29
Hatun Cuzqui, 87
haylyc, 95
headdress activity, 14–16
Heyerdahl, Thor, 104
highlands, 1–3, 22, 24
Hindi, 76
households, 7, 27–29, 76
Huacapata, 4
huacas, 32, 87
huairas, 67
Huascar, 5, 12
Huayna Capac, 5–6, 12
huay-yaya, 95
human sacrifices, 33–34, 63
hymns, 36

I Ilyap'a, 31
Inca by Privilege, 4
Inca empire, 3
Inca Roca, 12
Inca Urcon, 51
indigo dye, 44
inlaid objects, 67
Inti, 11, 13, 31, 32, 34–35, 55, 89
Inti Raymi, 87, 89
irrigation, 1, 22

J *jaillis,* 36
jewelry, 29
jobs, 7–8, 13, 23, 49, 53, 75–76
jugs
    description of, 62–63
    Portrait Jug activity, 63–65
jungle, 1–3

K kings
    burial customs for, 13, 30
    clothing of, 55
    headdress activity, 14–16
    heirs of, 11, 13
    lifestyle of, 12–13, 28, 39
    myths about, 5
    names of, 4–6, 12, 51, 82,
        98–99, 102
    power of, 3, 7, 11–13
    royal medallion activity, 16–17

Sapa Inca title of, 4, 12
Spanish Conquest of, 5–6
Kon-Tiki, 104

L labor. *See* jobs; *mit'a*
language
    plays/poetry, 49, 51–52
    Quechua, 3–6
laws, 8
litters, 11–13, 16
llamas
    for clothing, 42, 53, 54
    domestication of, 53, 61
    meat of, 39
    for rain ritual, 23
    sacrifice of, 33, 34, 87, 89
    silver llama figurine activity,
        68–71
    woven design activity, 56–61
llauta, 14
Lloque Ypanqui, 12
Llullaillaco, Mount, 63
looms, 53–54, 57
lower class, 4, 8, 24, 29
lunar calendar, 26

M Machu Picchu, 82
Magnificent Festival, 89
maguey plants, 81